COSMIC NEW YEAR

THOUGHTS FOR NEW YEAR 1920

5 Lectures Held in Stuttgart
December 21, 1919 – January 1, 1920

TRANSLATED BY PETER CLEMM
INTRODUCTION BY CHRISTOPHER BAMFORD

RUDOLF STEINER

SteinerBooks

CW 195

SteinerBooks
Anthroposophic Press

610 Main Street
Great Barrington, Massachusetts 01230
www.steinerbooks.org

Original translation from the German by Peter Clemm.

This book is volume 195 in the Collected Works (CW) of Rudolf Steiner, published by SteinerBooks, 2007. This is a translation of the German *Weltsilvester und Neujahrsgedanken* published by Rudolf Steiner Verlag, Dornach, Switzerland, 1993.

Library of Congress Cataloging-in-Publication Data

Steiner, Rudolf, 1861-1925.
  [Weltsilvester und Neujahrsgedanken. English]
  Cosmic new year : thoughts for new year 1920 : five lectures held in Stuttgart December 21, 1919-January 1, 1920 ; translated by Peter Clemm ; introduction by Christopher Bamford.
      p. cm. — (Collected works of Rudolf Steiner ; v. 195)
  Includes bibliographical references and index.
  ISBN 978-0-88010-613-9
  1. Anthroposophy. I. Title.

BP565.S7513 2007
299'.935–dc22

2007039245

Printed in the United States

COSMIC NEW YEAR

THOUGHTS FOR NEW YEAR 1920

RUDOLF STEINER (1923)

CONTENTS

3.

STUTTGART, DECEMBER 28, 1919

The mystery of the human will. The connection between the will and processes of destruction. Effects of the will and the course of nature. Lucifer's incarnation in ancient China. Eastern mysteries: their becoming abstract in Greek philosophy and fixed in phrases at the present time. The preparation for the incarnation of Ahriman. The erroneous interpretation of the Gospels as a means to prepare the incarnation of Ahriman.

4.

STUTTGART, DECEMBER 31, 1919

The relationship of human life to the past and the future regarded as a mirroring process. Perception of the "I" as a result of the interruption of consciousness during the night time. The necessity for the new revelation. The present day as a kind of Cosmic New Year. The necessity for a new experience of Christ. Gogarten's book *Spiritual Science and Christianity*. The attacks of the Jesuit Zimmermann. After the Cosmic New Year there must come a new year of the spiritual future.

5.

STUTTGART, JANUARY 1, 1920

Rudolf Steiner's early essay "The Spiritual Signature of the Present." Fichte and Hegel. The dogma of revelation and the dogma of mere sense experience. Lenin's social ideas. Spiritual science strives for a social order in which a balance exists between capacities and needs, i.e., between Lucifer and Ahriman. The characteristics of present East European culture (Lenin, Trotsky) with regard to the social sphere. In Middle Europe, the denial of the German spiritual life represented by Goethe and Schiller. Heinrich Deinhardt.

INTRODUCTION

CHRISTOPHER BAMFORD

Only those who absolutely will not look at what is happening in the world as a result of these last catastrophic years can close their eyes to the fact that we are starting out on the road to ruin, and that only something new can lead us away from this path. Whatever one may look for within this destructive process itself, it can never become anything else but a force of destruction. Now only what will really draw on sources that have not belonged to the Earth's development up till now can bring about a force for reconstruction.

(From Lecture Three)

1917, 1918, 1919, 1920 ... These were extraordinary years for Rudolf Steiner, Anthroposophy, and the world: dark, painful, tragic, socially chaotic times, filled with constant sudden reversals. Opportunities opened and closed with rapidity. Occasional lightning flashes of the spirit illuminated the gloom, but the situation never looked good. Nevertheless, despite the odds, a new age seemed possible. The Great War, which ended officially on November 11, 1918, had left Germany exhausted. The Versailles Peace Conference followed, opening on January 12, 1918. It had promised fairness and justice. But by the time it concluded its work on January 20, 1920, it had betrayed its noble intentions and stripped Germany of every shred of self-respect, leaving the country at the mercy of the most adversarial forces. Still, for a brief period, which continued as long as idealism could hold out, everything seemed possible. The stakes were the very highest, as the subsequent course of history demonstrates. To achieve anything one would have to work fast, intuitively, out of full cognizance of the spiritual realities of the moment. This Rudolf Steiner did with his whole being. Reading his lectures from this period, we find them marked by a particular sense of *urgency*.

Every one of Steiner's lectures occurs in particular context; and it is always difficult to know where to draw the boundaries in his life and work so as to place any given set of lectures into the context that best illuminates the spiritual atmosphere in and out of which he is talking. In the case of the five lectures printed here—which on the surface appear "occasional" and "interstitial"—we must go back to 1917.

At that moment, when the end of the War was only a matter of time, Steiner was among the most prescient. In anticipation of the inevitable peace—as the Bolshevik Revolution of November 1917 waited in the wings in Russia—he met in Berlin with a German diplomat, Otto von Lerchenfeld, to prepare a counter strategy. Two *Memoranda* resulted, outlining a radically new vision of socio-political, economic, and cultural life for post-War Germany. Steiner called his new approach "threefold"—he would speak of the need to "threefold" society or the "threefolding" of society.

Twenty-seven years of research (from 1882 to 1917) had just provided convincing evidence that the human being was composed of three systems—a bodily or metabolic system, a soul or respiratory/circulatory system, and a nerve-sense (spirit) system—with three functions (willing, feeling, and thinking). He announced these findings most succinctly in the sixth appendix to *Riddles of the Soul* (CW 21), published in November 1917. Now, drawing on other spiritual research, he proposed that human society was also threefold, and composed of three different orders of activity that we may call the economic, legal-rights, and spiritual-cultural spheres. Reinterpreting the motto of the French Revolution—*Liberté, Egalité, Fraternité,* Steiner proposed that each sphere of activity should operate according to different principles: "fraternity" (or association) in the economic sphere, "equality" in the legal-rights sphere, and "freedom" in the spiritual-cultural sphere.

Although the *Memoranda* were read widely and in the highest circles, nothing came of them. Once the War was over, and the ensuing chaos set in, it was clear to Steiner that what they contained must be taken up in a practical way. This meant that Anthroposophy would have to transform itself to engage its mission in a new way. World evolution now called for initiation knowledge—spiritual science—to engage society directly. The esoteric would have to become exoteric. Consequently, Anthroposophy, as the years unfolded, would be increasingly in the glare of public scrutiny, continuously open to criticism, and even attack.

The years following the end of the War thus gave rise to a series of social and spiritual initiatives, whose success would depend not only on Steiner's ability to convince the public but also on his ability to convince Anthroposophists as a body to unite in the pursuit of these goals. To reach the general public, the spiritual-scientific epistemology and insights had to be translated into accessible, jargon-free, ordinary language that educated people could understand. For many of the older members the shift proved divisive. They had difficulty recognizing the new language of Anthroposophy. At the same time, the situation demanded that everyone concerned develop the presence of mind to act with dedication and responsibility. It was a struggle on two fronts, internal and external. It was not clear which was the easier task. Both proved equally difficult.

1919, then, saw the beginning of the work to make "The Movement for the Threefolding of the Social Organism" into a popular, political movement. November 1918 had seen the German Revolution. Socialist (Social Democrat) in orientation, almost bloodless in its unfolding (only fifteen people died), it would pave the way for the future Weimar Republic. Communists, socialists, conservatives, and nationalists continued to foment for their causes. Legitimate political groups, as well as gangs of thugs, roamed the streets in search of supporters. It was a desperate time. Anything could still happen—and did, as history, unfortunately, was to show. Steiner and his co-workers made heroic efforts (including almost daily meetings with workers, managers, owners, as well as finance ministers and other powerful people) to bring the threefold idea into the public forum. They had some initial success, but, in the long run, the odds were against them. There was too much confusion, and too many competing philosophies and ideologies.

Out of the Threefold Movement, however, on the initiative of Emil Molt, owner of the Waldorf Astoria Cigarette Factory in Stuttgart, the first Waldorf School was created for the factory workers' children.

The idea was born in November of the previous year; ten months later, on September 7, 1919, the doors were opened. Before they did so, in the two weeks preceding, Steiner gave his first specifically "Waldorf" lectures—the foundational cycle *The Foundations of Human Experience* (or "The Study of Man") (CW 293)—based on the now established reality of the threefoldness of the developing human being. The threefold seed had thus germinated the foundation of cultural renewal through education. At the same time, other initiatives, exemplary of the threefold idea were also planned.

1919 witnessed another, most profound moment. At the end of November in Dornach, Steiner gave the seminal lectures (published in *The Archangel Michael: His Mission and Ours*) on "The Mission of Michael and the new Michael Revelation" (CW 194). Therewith, Anthroposophy explicitly became a "School of Michael."

The doctrine of the archangelic regents of human evolution in periods of 354 years had been part of esoteric lore at least since Trithemius's *Treatise on the Seven Secondary Causes, or Spirits Who Move the Spheres According to God* (1515). According to this tradition, the Archangel Michael assumed the guidance of humanity in 1879. Steiner had long alluded to the enormous significance of this fact, which was coupled in his mind with the end of the Kali Yuga or "Age of Iron" in 1900; and although, in a certain sense, he had always placed his work at the service of Michael, he had to wait for the right moment to proclaim the full import of the "Michaelic Age." This moment started in 1917 and with the end of the War achieved an earnest and near-overwhelming urgency. For he understood that it was only in service to Michael—only in becoming truly students and companions of Michael, and thoroughly permeating oneself with the "Michaelic" consciousness that leads to Christ—that a truly new culture was possible. Only Michael could ensure the proper "enchristing" of consciousness that the times demanded. As Steiner said in his second lecture (November 22):

> Michael is the spirit of strength. With his entrance into human evolution, he must make it possible for us to get beyond the point of having, on the one hand, an abstract spirituality and on the

other a material world that can be hammered on and dissected without our having conception that it, too, is a manifestation of the spirit. Michael must penetrate us as the strength, the force who can see through matter to the spirit everywhere present in it....We must see to it that human beings take up the spiritual, not just into their head, but into their whole being. We must permeate ourselves wholly with the spiritual. Only the Christ can help us do that. But Michael must help in interpreting the Christ to us. Then we will be able to add to the words of the Evangelist the following: *"And the time must come when the flesh will again become the Word and learn to dwell in the kingdom of the Word."*

Such then is the general context of the lectures given over New Year 1919-1920 and published here.

✳

The specific context is an extended visit to Stuttgart. Steiner had been visiting throughout the year in preparation for the creation of the Waldorf School, lecturing on social and pedagogic questions (CW 192). This time he arrived on December 18. The next day, he gave a public lecture on "Spiritual Science: Freedom of Thought and Social Forces." His theme was the connection between thinking and willing—headwork and handwork—as the foundation for freedom and spiritual research. The next two days, he visited classes in the new Free Waldorf School, which was just ending its first semester, and, on the following day, spoke at the School's Christmas festival. That same evening (December 21), he gave the first of the lectures to members collected here (the others falling on December 25, 28, and 31 to end January 1, 1920.) In between, he met with teachers and—astonishingly—gave *two* lecture courses! It had previously been arranged that, over the Christmas break (December 23 to January 3), he would give a science course for science teachers and other invited people. The first of three science courses, it had been announced as *The Light Course* (CW 320). (*The Warmth Course* [CW 321] and *The Astronomy Course* [CW 322] would follow.) Steiner would improvise this course. But at the same time, at the last moment, some teachers had asked him to give another course—on language. And so he gave *The Genius of Language* (CW 299). As if this were not enough, as all this lecturing and counseling activity was going on, meetings were held on the founding of a business, *Der Kommende Tag* ("The Coming Day"), which would exemplify threefold principles. On December 27 and 30, two more public lectures (both (CW 333) were given: "The Cosmic Balance of Soul and Spirit Life Today" and "Spiritual Knowledge as the Foundation for Action—Ethics in Knowing—Human Hope from Spiritual Power." Finally, on New Years Eve, after his lecture, Steiner was sitting with Emil Molt. Molt asked whether he would accept the Chairmanship of the new company. As Steiner said, "Yes," the bells began to peal, announcing the New Year. That, too, would be a busy one.

✳

Truly, Rudolf Steiner's effort on our behalf—"to impress something new into the development of humanity"—was almost super-human. As stated, *Cosmic New Year* was one of three courses that he gave at the same time. No wonder that, at the close of the final lecture, he had to conclude with the following most moving personal remarks:

My dear friends, during this present short visit every day is so filled up from morning to evening because there is so much to inaugurate, to accomplish, to arrange, that it is not possible this time for one to consider all the requests that have come to me. I can only say on the one hand: since not everything can happen that should happen, therefore I will return again in the not-too-distant future, and then personal requests can be taken care of. But I also ask that you take this into your consideration as well. Not everything can be done in a few days, in a few days in which greater arrangements also have to be made, in which I am also worried about our Waldorf School, which should now have a deep impact in a new way on the development of humanity. It is therefore also not possible to consider all the private requests, since, as you can see, I am having a difficulty in speaking. It is not a cold—it is the same as you feel when you have been chopping wood all day long, it is nothing more than an over-tiredness of the vocal cords that can then more easily catch cold. But today it is necessary above all else to look at what is necessary for the service of humankind as a whole. And forgive me therefore that this time individual requests cannot be honored.

*

Cosmic New Year, then, consists of five lectures, given to members of the Anthroposophical Society in Stuttgart, and reflecting the various concerns and themes of the hour. They convey the urgency Rudolf Steiner felt both about the issues and the need to understand them. Not only were the issues of supreme moment in themselves, it was also vitally important that the "ordinary" membership both support them and take them up in their own lives. With the proliferation of social, educational, artistic, and other initiatives, he knew that it was imperative that members come together in their support. Otherwise, division, fragmentation, and spiritual bankruptcy would follow. At the same time, since they are members—and because he is squeezing these lectures in between others and a continuous stream of meetings, they have an intimate, open tone: Steiner is speaking person-to-person and face-to-face. Such indeed was always his relation to the membership. It was an ongoing, deep relationship. Therefore Steiner is always aware in speaking of the last encounter or conversation. He picks up, as it were, where he left off, thus affirming a consciousness of unity.

*

The tone, nevertheless, is one of urgency. The times are dire. Initiation knowledge—the fruit of spiritual-scientific research—can no longer afford to remain the private precinct of esotericists. The chaos into which the War's ending had thrown Europe—revealing the bankruptcy of the old values and modes of thinking that had led to the conflict in the first place—provided a unique opportunity for a new spiritually inspired way of being to reconstruct society on quite different grounds. It was a gift that should be returned. Anthroposophists, who had grown used to the comfort of their spiritual "club," must therefore begin to understand that they had a larger mission: to bring a truly Michaelic consciousness into the public arena.

Thus, he begins by reaffirming that the time demands that initiation knowledge flow into cultural development. But why is this so difficult? It is difficult, he says, because people fear spiritual knowledge. They are afraid of it. They are terrified of it because inwardly—even if unconsciously—they know that spiritual reality underlies all their thinking. Yet if they were to admit it, all their avowed assumptions about the world would collapse. Everything they thought was reality would become an image, a trace. If they were brave enough, they would realize that another path, another way of knowing, was necessary. And it is only this other way of knowing—out of the supersensible—that can "enlighten us about everything that surrounds us today in such a chaotic and devastating way."

And so the first lecture turns to its main theme: the three life streams that make up human cultural life—spiritual life, economic life, and legal life or the life of rights. Steiner begins with spiritual life, which, he says, comes to us from Greece, whither it arrived from the East, from the centers of "The Mysteries of Light," or the Spirit. From these ancient Indian mystery centers radiated an initiation knowledge that permeated the whole of life. After millennia, this knowledge finally reached Greece, but when it did, it was but a mere shadow of what it had been before. The original clairvoyance of the founding period had faded. Intellect more and more took its place until, today, it rules as abstract intellectuality, pervading the streams of legal and economic life with which it is wound or tangled up like a "ball of yarn." "Legal" life, as Steiner tells it, for its part, arose in ancient Egypt, in the "Human Mysteries." Passing through Rome, it took on an unimaginative legalistic quality, which in turn affected religious life also: it too became legalistic, unimaginative, and intellectual. Social life, meanwhile, originated "more in the North," taking on its hardened, intellectual form in "Anglo-American social organization," whose philosophical consequences we find in philosophers like Newton, Hume, Darwin, Mill, and Spencer. Today, these three threads are completely entangled one with another and permeated with dead materialistic intellectualism. Spiritual science can and must show the way out.

Such, in brief, is the essential content of the first lecture. Several "asides," however, dropped in the course of the main argument and not followed up, are worth noting, for they will reverberate through what is to come. Christ, for instance, is mentioned, clearly as part of any solution, but not expanded on. But a seed is planted. Related to this, Steiner briefly invokes Theosophy more harshly than usual, as an attempt at re-spiritualization that was part of the problem rather than any solution: colonizing Indian wisdom it created a hybrid spirituality with an Anglo-American (materialist) coloring. Also interesting from a human and historical perspective is Steiner's response to the criticism and attacks on Anthroposophy and his person as a consequence of taking spiritual science into the public arena. He does not take it personally, yet clearly feels that every attack should be forcefully answered. He does not take the high road of being above the fray, but engages the opposition with passion.

The second, Christmas (December 25), lecture makes clear—if one doubted—the relevance of this now apparently distant period to our own. How, Steiner asks, can we celebrate such festivals, and not forget "all the pain and suffering of this time" and "all the manifestations of the decline which is taking hold of humanity in our present culture"? Surely, this question has only increased in urgency since Steiner first asked it.

How do we turn to the Christ in the right way today? Steiner answers this question, after detailing many symptoms of the false view of Christianity prevalent everywhere, by turning to the other great theme of the moment: the Archangel Michael. Michael is now—since 1879—not only the Regent of humanity and, specifically, the guide and teacher of spiritual science in our time, he is also now "the countenance of Christ Jesus," as he had previously, before

Golgotha, been the countenance of Yahweh. Too many people still relate to him atavistically in the old way: they still place the nation, the folk, above the individual. (Here the allusion is to Woodrow Wilson, and the debacle of the Versailles Peace Treaty, which took its stand on "independence for even the smallest nations" so, in this context is quintessentially Luciferic, or atavistic.) Seeking Christ, whose face is Michael, is something else: it is the universal human, which is approached through the conscious inward striving for the truth, as is made possible through spiritual science. Michael seeks to aid us in this, but he is not alone in inclining toward us. We must also navigate between the Scylla and Charybdis of Lucifer and Ahriman, the one tempting us toward a kind of pre-Golgotha relation to Christ as some kind of transcendent deity, the other tempting us to a Gospel fundamentalism that denies a living soul relation to Christ (and Michael). Christ must live between Lucifer and Ahriman, between these temptations, as a paradoxical "middle way" between transcendence and materialism.

The remaining lectures then take up and, always with a sense of urgency, develop these themes: the need for initiation knowledge; the three streams of cultural life; Lucifer and Ahriman and how to work with them; the Michael-Christ revelation; and, above all, the need to constantly strive for the truth.

Truth, indeed, as Steiner uses it is a key, unifying idea. For truth, finally, is what takes hold of us, claims us, penetrates us, and grows in us, transforming us. It is the very opposite of either an intellectualistic, disembodied (Luciferic) or a materialist (Ahrimanic) approach. It does not have to do with certainty, but with living, transformative, and revelatory experience. It is truth in this sense that must be stood up for—no matter whom it offends.

Truths of this kind, he tells us in his New Year's Eve lecture, should become the content of the "I," now empty and devoid of ancient clairvoyance, and "more or less only a point." This point must become a circle as the "truths" of spiritual science enter into us and lay their claim upon us. Most importantly, such living truths are of the future. They come from the Christ and out of them the future will grow. It is this that makes New Year a cosmic or world New Year.

For such living truths, reconnecting humanity with the suprasensory world and the divine, available since 1879, are the gifts of Michael. But we must receive them in a living way and create through living and communicating them a new kind of community—to which, of course, there will be great opposition from those still petrified in the past.

All in all, this is an extraordinarily rich, dense little sequence of lectures, amounting essentially to "a call to awaken." In this spirit, he concludes his New Year's Day lecture:

> I would very much wish that a New Year's resolution that each person can only make for themselves will be there among us: namely, that through the hearts and minds of our friends eyes are opened for the vision of what is desperately needed, opened for what can only come from the spirit alone in order to help humanity. Today we cannot bring about healing with the existing outer arrangements; we must impress something new into the development of humanity.

So it was in 1920; so it is still today.

COSMIC NEW YEAR

THOUGHTS FOR NEW YEAR 1920

Rudolf Steiner

Lecture 1

STUTTGART, DECEMBER 21, 1919

T HOSE of you who attended the last lectures held here[†] will now understand that it is a demand of our time to let the so-called science of initiation, the true science of the spiritual life, flow into today's cultural development. I have also described what hindrances stand in the way of spiritual science flowing into both the cultural life of the present and that of the future.

Above all else, in the world today there is what I have often characterized as the fear of spiritual knowledge. One only has to say this and people nowadays pretend to be offended.

For how, according to some people, at a time when we have come so wonderfully far, could people have any kind of fear of knowledge? Indeed, people today believe they are able to encompass nearly everything with their intellectual powers. But people are not generally conscious of this fear that I have often described. In their consciousness people pretend that they are brave enough to receive every kind of knowledge, but deep in the unknown part of the soul (which today people basically don't want to acknowledge) there sits this unconscious fear. Because these people have this unconscious fear, there rise up in them all kinds of reasons that they claim to be logical objections against spiritual science. However, they are only emanations of the unconscious fear of the science of the spirit that reigns in human souls. For in the depths of the soul every human being really knows much more than is known intellectually. We do not want this knowledge rooted in the depths of the soul life to rise to consciousness, because we are just afraid of it. Above all else, the human being divines this about the supersensible worlds: in everything we call thinking, in everything in the world of thoughts, something of the supersensible world can be found.

Even materialistically minded people of today cannot always rid themselves of the suspicion that something is indeed contained in the life of thought that points somehow to a supersensible world. But at the same time people also suspect something else about this world of thought: that this thought life is related to actual reality in the same way an image seen in a mirror is related to the reality being reflected. And just as the image in the mirror is actually nothing real, so the human being should also admit that the thought world is not a reality. In the moment that the human being had the courage, the fearlessness, to admit that the thought world is not real, the person would also be seized by a longing to know the spiritual world. For we surely would like to know what is actually real behind what we only see as a reflected image.

But now I must point out that what I have just said has an important polar opposite. If by means of spiritual science we cross the threshold into the supersensible, then everything we experience here as sensible reality is transformed to a mere picture, an apparent image. Just as here on the Earth the supersensible world is a mirror image, so is the earthly world only present as a mirror image in the supersensible world. If we speak out of the science of initiation, we must therefore of course speak of sensible reality only as pictures. When we speak this way, people feel that the world—where they can stand so comfortably, breathe in so comfortably, see so comfortably without having to do anything about it, except at most to open their eyes in the morning and to rub them a bit—is just turned into a picture. When people feel this, they begin to feel unsafe; they begin to feel about as unsafe as someone who has come to the edge of an abyss and is seized by dizziness and fear.

On the one hand, a person would have to feel that thinking here in the sense world is merely a collection of images, and on the other, would have to feel (but gets over it because of the unconscious fear) that what tells of a supersensible world makes this world into an image.

Now of course not everyone today can easily experience what someone who enters directly into the world of initiation has to go through. Those entering the world of initiation must not only recognize what all people today should strive to recognize, but they must also live in it; they must live in it the way one lives with one's body in the physical sense world. That means they must actually, so to speak, as a substitute experience what one goes through in the physical sense world at the moment of death. They must become able to live in a world for which the physical-sensory human being is not suited at all. Even when we only cut our finger a little we feel a certain pain, an uncomfortable feeling. Why do we feel something uncomfortable when we cut our finger? Well, for the simple reason that the knife certainly cuts into the skin, muscle, and nerve, but not into the supersensible etheric body. When the finger has not been cut, then our etheric body matches the uncut finger. When we have cut the finger but cannot cut the etheric body, then the etheric body no longer matches the cut finger and therefore the astral body feels pain. The pain comes from the mismatch with the physical corporeality. When the human being steps across the threshold of the supersensible world, then the physical body is no longer attached to all the other bodies; then the person gradually feels in a larger way something like what is felt after a finger is cut. And this, my dear friends, this we must imagine the person feeling to an unlimited degree.

Now of course one can hardly imagine what would come over people of the present day—who are often so brave in their consciousness, often so woeful in their souls—if they were suddenly to be able to live in the supersensible world, and if they had to endure all that comes from being unfitted for this supersensible world. Present-day humanity has come so far that they can comprehend everything related by those who know about the life in the supersensible, and this is an absolute necessity for the healthy human understanding of the present day. For only the knowledge of the supersensible can enlighten us about everything surrounding us today in such a chaotic and devastating way. Indeed we live in a world where we must say about the things that appear and occur:

they cannot continue to be, they must undergo a transformation. But present-day humanity cannot at all see through what actually lives around them, because one can only see in this way through the knowledge of initiation. One can only do it by being able, above all else, to compare the life of the present with all the influences that in the course of centuries, of millennia, have deeply affected the development of humanity.

At a certain point in time it had to be said publicly: the one fruitful impulse we need to bring into human life, which is beset by such destructive phenomena today, is none other than the threefolding of the social realm.† By saying this, human souls were directed to the three basic streams of social life of the present time: the true cultural life, the political-rights life, and the outer economic life. A great number of life's phenomena are encompassed within each one of these basic streams. Let us then allow these streams to briefly pass before our mind's eye one after the other.

Today we have a spiritual life, in which the human being participates in various ways. One individual may only attend a public school, based on his or her economic or legal life circumstances, while another may advance further in our institutions of learning. What people absorb in those places lives with us as part of our social life. This is what determines our relationship to our fellow human beings. Now is the time when one must in a profound way bring up the question: where then does this whole spiritual life come from, and how in the course of its development has it assumed the exact character it has today? If one traces back to the true origin of our spiritual life, then one must first pass through certain stations, so to speak. What prevails today in the life of our public schools, in the life of higher education, all harkens back to the distant past (I will omit the in-between stations).

Usually one does not know where the public school system originated; for example, one does not realize that it goes back to what arose in ancient Greece.

Basically our spiritual life is nourished by impulses that lived in ancient Greece in a somewhat different form, which have only transformed themselves since then. But they also arose in the East and then had (several millennia ago, to be sure) a different form than they already had in ancient Greece. In those days in the East, the impulses were mystery wisdom. If we leave out our political-rights life, which is chaotically tangled up like a ball with the spiritual life, and leave out the economic life—if we separate out our spiritual life in an abstract way, then we can trace the way back thousands of years to certain mysteries of the East. In these mysteries there was something altogether alive, while the educational institutions of today have a lifeless character and teach only dry, prosaic abstractions. If we transport ourselves back in the spirit to those mysteries of the East, then we meet human beings presiding over these mysteries whom we can describe as a kind of combination of priest and king, and at the same time—strange as it may sound to people today—of economist and manager. For in these mysteries—I want to call them Mysteries of the Light or of the Spirit—an all-encompassing knowledge of life was practiced, a knowledge of life that was aimed both at investigating the being of the human being out of the world of the heavens and the stars and at regulating the lawful community life of people in the light of the above-gained knowledge. From these mystery centers directions were given out how to care for cattle, how to plant the fields, how to build canals, and so forth. This initiation knowledge of ancient times had a powerful social impact—it filled the whole human being, and was something that did not simply say nice things about what was good and true, but was in a position to control, organize, and shape practical life out of the spirit. The path these leaders of the mysteries followed and that, as far as they could, they showed to the people connected to these mysteries, was a way from above downward. First these leaders of the mysteries strove to reveal the spiritual worlds, and then they worked downward in that they concretely took hold of the spirit according to the basic principles of the atavistic art of clairvoyance. They worked down into the political life, to the political structuring of the social organisms, all the way to economics and commerce. That was wisdom with life impact. How did this wisdom actually come about in humanity?

If we go back to the times when these mysteries were not yet authoritative, in the regions of civilized humanity there were many people with a certain primitive atavistic clairvoyance—people who, when they spoke of what they needed for their life, could depend on the impressions of their heart, their soul, their seeing. These people were spread out over the regions of today's India, Persia, Armenia, North Africa, southern Europe and so on. But one thing did not live in the souls of these people, what today we regard as our proudest soul capacity: intelligence or understanding. Understanding was not yet needed, so to speak, by the population of the then civilized world. For what is done through intelligence today was then done out of the people's soul inspirations and was led and guided by their leaders. But into just those regions there spread out what we could call another race, what we could call an entirely different kind of human being than the population of which we are speaking.

In the sagas, myths, and in history as well, it is said that in very ancient times people came down from the highlands of Asia who brought a certain culture to the south and southwest. Spiritual science must determine what kind of people these were, who came down to those people who received the directing force for their lives only out of their inspirations, from within. We find through spiritual science that these people, who came into the civilization of that time like a new element of the population, combined two things that the others did not have. The other people had atavistic clairvoyance without understanding, without intelligence; those who came down also still had some clairvoyance, but at the same time they had the initial basis for intelligence and understanding. These are the first Aryans, as described by history. The first caste distinctions (at that time external, physical, empirical in nature) first arose from the antithetical relation between the old, atavistically inclined souls and those whose soul forces were penetrated by understanding—distinctions that still have their aftereffects in Asia, and about which Tagore[†] speaks, for example. The most eminent of these incoming people, who had at the same time the old clairvoyance and the understanding and intelligence just then arising in humanity, became the leaders of those Mysteries of the Eastern Light, and from them proceeded what later developed in Greece. So that, sketching it out schematically, I can say to you: from the East the spirit streamed forth.

Mysteries

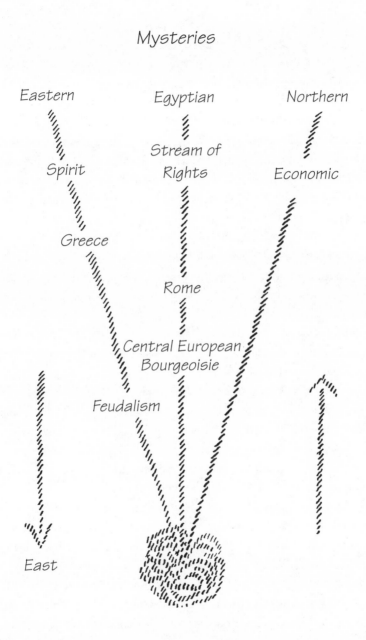

Current Culture

It was a living wisdom with a practical life-impulse. In the course of time it came over to Greece, and we still perceive its aftereffects in the earliest Greek culture. But in the progress of Greek culture it becomes, so to speak, filtered, thinned out, as the bearers of the culture lose the old clairvoyance and the intellect takes its place ever more and more. As a result the culture bearers thereby lose their significance, because they are significant only because they are simultaneously endowed with both clairvoyance and intelligence. But in history it happens that something that was significant in ancient times lives on into a later time, and so in the cultural life of Greece the people continue to live equipped, so to speak, with what was significant for that former time, when the leaders of the mysteries were like envoys of the gods. And so what formerly was a wisdom with impulsive strength was transformed into Greek logic and dialectic, into the Greek wisdom that has already been filtered down when compared with what was once its Eastern source.

At the time of that wisdom's Eastern origin, one knew exactly why there were people who paid attention when the leaders gave their directions in the field of economics, but in Greece it had become a division into masters and slaves. The division between people still existed, but its deeper significance was gradually lost. The Greeks still had something of much greater significance that they at least knew came from the old mysteries, but that was filtered down even more on its way into our cultural life of recent times. For there, in our recent cultural life, it has become completely abstract. Today we deal in abstract knowledge and do not find a connection anymore between this abstract knowledge and outer life. This cultural current came through Greece and proceeded into our colleges, high schools, and elementary schools, and into the whole popular spiritual life of modern humanity. And today we can observe a peculiar phenomenon: among the people who wander around us today we meet those whom we call the nobility or aristocrats. We endeavor in vain to find a reason why one is an aristocrat and the other is not, because the ability to recognize the difference between an aristocrat and a non-aristocrat has long been lost by humanity. The aristocrats were the leaders of the Eastern Mysteries of the Light, and they could be this because from them emanated everything that had a real life-impulse in the political and economic life. This wisdom has been filtered—the structure it had brought about among people had become an abstraction, without any sense for those standing within it, and from this abstraction arose what we call feudalism. In the outer social life this feudalism is tolerated, perhaps also irritating those others for whom it makes no sense. One does not think anymore about its sense, because it is not found in the life of today, but in the chaos of the present time the feudal origin of our abstract knowledge and learning is still quite apparent. When our contemporary spiritual life then became entirely a life of journalism, an expression was invented (truly a word monstrosity) that was intended to bring about a transformation of our life, but that has only become a description of our completely rachitic spiritual life: "spiritual aristocracy." Spiritual aristocracy! If someone wanted to explain what is actually meant by that, then one could only say: it is what used to have strong impact in all areas of practical life in the Eastern mysteries, which made sense then but is now totally squeezed out and has no sense whatever today. If one wanted to make a picture of our spiritual life now, then one would have to draw a tangled-up ball of wool down there, where the three threads are so tangled up together (see figure p. 7).

It is our essential task to disentangle this ball, and for that we turn our soul's attention to the second cultural stream. This second stream has a different origin, which also lies far back in the evolution of humanity but which originates in the actual being of the mysteries, namely in the mysteries of Egypt. Having called the Eastern mysteries the Mysteries of the Light, I would like to call these the Mysteries of the Human Being. These mysteries attempted above all else to gain the wisdom from their Egyptian origin that gives the capacity to bring structure into human community life, to formulate a basis for the relationship of people to one another. But this mystery stream then spread out and up through southern Europe (just as the other one did through Greece) and found its way through to the Romans, a people lacking in fantasy. I would like to call it the Stream of the Law. Everything that in the course of human development has gradually been cultivated as jurisprudence, as determination of rights—*that* is the filtered knowledge, the filtered perception of these Mysteries of the Human Being.

The second thread within our cultural ball has reached all the way to us, but very, very changed, very metamorphosed, having passed through Rome and its absence of fantasy. We cannot understand contemporary life if we do not see that so far human beings have remained unfruitful for the life of the spirit and the life of rights, if we do not see that humanity received the spiritual life after it had made the long journey to us from the Eastern mysteries through Greece, and the rights life after it made the long journey to us from the mysteries of Egypt by way of Rome. One could point to many phenomena that would be proof of contemporary humanity's unfruitfulness, but we need only look at the path taken by Christianity.

When it was time for Christianity to appear upon the Earth, where did Christ Jesus have to appear, so that what he had to give to the world would find a way? He had to appear in the East; he had to place what he had to give to humanity into what lived in the East. The Mystery of Golgotha is a fact; what people know about it is still developing. What was said about the Mystery of Golgotha was clothed initially in everything that still remained from the Mysteries of the East.

The Mystery of Golgotha was surrounded by the knowledge and wisdom of the Eastern mysteries, and people attempted to understand it with this wisdom. That is about how we still find Christianity at the time of the Greek church teachers.

One can also point to still another phenomenon. When the completely spiritually barren Western culture sought for spiritual refreshment in the person of one of its representatives, what did it do? Some people from England and America got together and took the wisdom from the defeated and enslaved folk of India. That is, they recently went over to the East to search for what had remained as a last remnant of that spiritual stream. Hence it was Theosophy, with an Anglo-American coloring, which wanted to draw from this source, but in its current condition. It is the barren state of contemporary spiritual life† that stands out most strongly just in the Western countries.

And the second stream is the one that has a political-legal character, which went through Rome, and is the origin of our life of
political rights. This stream only flowed into our legal system through
a side branch, and continues to work in it so that in many ways what
flowed into our culture in the form of spiritual life was received in
a roundabout way from the Roman political-juridical system. Even
Christianity, which spread itself out in the West under Roman influence, took on the form that was determined by it.

What then has become of the religious element as a result of
passing through the transition point of Rome? It has become the great
jurisprudence called the Roman Catholic religion. There God, with
his lesser gods, is altogether a being who rules according to Roman
legal concepts, only in the supersensible world. The concepts of sin
and guilt are stuck in there, which are actually judicial concepts that
were not contained in the Mysteries of the East or in the Greek view
of life—these are judicial concepts of the Romans. It is a religious
stream totally tied up in legalisms. Everything that is expressed in life
can also take on a beautiful form. And so when we see this judicial-
political scene, with the World God become a World Judge and the
whole of world development finalized by a judicial act, beautifully
glorified by the paintings of Michelangelo in the Sistine Chapel, it
is the glorious expression of a Christianity tied up in legalisms—a
legalistically tied-up Christianity that finds its crowning moment in
the Last Judgment.

We must unravel the tangled-up ball of our spiritual life and
political and rights life in order to see what is contained in it, because
being in it we live in a cultural chaos. These streams have their influence on us, and we must disentangle them. But yet a third stream
has flowed into our cultural tangle, which took its origin more from
the North and which up to now has been primarily preserved (also
filtered, but in another direction) in the Anglo-American social organization. I would like to call this the Mysteries of the North, or the
Mysteries of the Earth. What developed first of all as primitive spirituality from the Mysteries of the Earth is a different way than that
taken by the spiritual element in the East. There it took the way from
above to below—first revealing itself as the Mysteries of the Heavens

and the Light, then carried down into the political and economic sphere. Here in the North, things developed out of the economy. This origin has, to be sure, disappeared from outer life; at best it can still be noticed in some old remnants that have still survived. Take, for example, such customs that are still described when speaking of the old Northern culture, of which England is a part. There at a certain time of year you find processions going through the villages with a crowned bull, whose task it will be to fructify the cows. In this a longing for the spiritual life was brought out from below to above. There everything, even what was there of primitive spirituality, was based on the economic life, and all festivals originally expressed something of the purpose of the economic life. Just as in the Eastern culture the way was made from above to below, so must the way here in the North be made from below to above. Humanity must be raised up from below, from the economy up through the life of rights into the mysteries of the spirit. But you see, this way from below to above has still not progressed very far. If we examine the way the judicial life has developed in the Western countries, we find it is entirely oriented according to Rome. If we examine the spiritual life, we often find it (not as obviously) characterized by its Eastern origin, as in the Indian Theosophy I spoke of earlier. However we do find what is contained there as original spiritual life, which was not imported from the East or legalistically from Rome, trying hard to separate itself out of the economic life. Let us take a characteristic case.

We can only understand such philosophers, such investigators of nature as Newton, Darwin, Mill, Spencer, and Hume,[†] when we see how they developed above and beyond the economic life, how they tried to find the way upwards. For example, we can only understand Mill as a national economist if we explain him as being beyond the economic fundamentals that surrounded him. We can only understand the English philosophers, if we explain them as being above these economic fundamentals as well. This is something attached to the third stream, the stream of the Mysteries of the Earth, which streams from below upwards and which, still quite inexplicably, has woven itself into our modern civilized life as the third thread in our ball.

There you have the three threads that live in our so-called civilized life chaotically woven together in a ball. In a certain way people have always risen up against this. Least of all in the West; there and in America, the economic life that came from the Mysteries of the North was embraced, and on this were built theories that were foreign to and devoid of the spirit, though built scientifically. The juristic-political-rights life was taken up via the roundabout way through Rome, and the spiritual life element from the East. In Middle Europe resistance rose up against this from many quarters. There, in many ways people strove to apprehend these things in their purity—most intensively in the spiritual life that I would like to call Goetheanism. Goethe, who wanted to eliminate jurisprudence from natural science, is characteristic of the uprising against the merely Eastern spiritual life. Because just as in Christianity, we also have jurisprudence in natural science: we speak of laws of nature. Those from the East did not speak of laws of nature, but of the rule of the Cosmic Will. Laws of nature only arose when the Roman side-stream was taken up. There the judicial law crept in through a window into the perception of nature and became law of nature. Goethe wanted to grasp hold of the pure appearance, the pure fact, the pure phenomenon—the archetypal phenomenon. Unless we cleanse our natural science from the appendages of jurisprudence, we will not achieve a cleansed spiritual life. Therefore spiritual science everywhere takes hold of facts, and only points out laws as secondary phenomena.

Then we also find a certain opposition to the Roman legal system, which is also found sticking in the heads of those oriented towards socialism: for instance—yes, even a Prussian minister of education—in Wilhelm von Humboldt.† When he wrote his beautiful essay on the limits of the state's activity, there lived in him something of the urge to thrust the cultural and economic life away from that of the state. Read the lovely little Reclam booklet (I don't know what it costs today, it used to be available for a few pennies) *Ideas Towards an Attempt to Determine the Limits of the Activity of the State*. There lives the urge to extract the legal-political activities out of the other two. This uprising against the old lives in German philosophy as well. But health and healing can come into this cultural development of humanity only if we develop a healthy view of what the knowledge of initiation can give us concerning the origin of our cultural life.

Particularly in Eastern Europe, perception takes place through the feelings, and there one always perceived the necessity of the three elements living together in our present cultural life. For of these three streams, what came from the North came to expression most characteristically in the West. There the economic life drowns out everything else. We can see the legal aspects particularly in Central Europe, and we find a great deal of the Mysteries of the East, of the Light, in Eastern Europe and in Asia. There, where we still come across the caste system, we still find something of the idea of the old feudalism coming from the spirit. Life penetrated by law has bred the modern bourgeoisie—the bourgeoisie comes from the legal stream. Today one must clearly see through these things. I would like to say: subconsciously people have the urge to see through such things, but only spiritual science can bring real clarity to this urge, this longing. It always also showed itself in the nineteenth century, how people strove to arrive at ideals for the future through the intermingling of often unclear currents. One wanted to achieve this by not having people face one another abstractly—they do so today because the life of the spirit and the life of rights has been filtered and lives in us in an abstract way, and the economic life pants along behind to find the way from below upwards.

In Eastern Europe, where so many significant and devastating things are taking place—there this longing first showed itself when people tried to deal with this cultural entanglement by rising up against it. The Russian revolutionaries[†] of the second and last third of the nineteenth century tried to fructify what had been left behind in the East and still contained a certain preliminary stage of the cultural life. They tried to fructify it with what appeared in Middle Europe as an uprising against what was handed down from olden times. And so in the letters exchanged by Russian revolutionaries of the second and last third of the nineteenth century we see how they actually point out that already in Middle Europe the intellect, the pure merely abstract life of reason, has tried to penetrate itself with a certain spirituality. And ever and again amongst these Russian revolutionaries something arises that can be expressed thus: in German philosophy it was attempted to uplift the intellect, which had lost the old clairvoyance, to a certain spirituality once again. In the East one wanted to become intimately familiar with what had arisen in Middle Europe, and the intimacy was reflected in the way these revolutionaries wrote. They very much revered the philosopher Ivan Petrovitch and spoke about how he had raised himself to purity of thought, how he had tried to bring the spirit once again into the dialectical thought games of Western culture, and they tried to draw conclusions from his philosophy. In order to express more fully their feeling relationship to him, they call him, not Hegel, "*the* Ivan Petrovitch." Just in these efforts we see a preliminary ghostly vision, I would like to say, of what was later destined to become devastating. In our time there must be clarity over the whole Earth. Therefore everything must be done to help this clarity achieve victory. But if the effort is made to come to this clarity, we must become aware of all we are up against today: the need of people to feel comfortable, besides many other things. We must get out of the habit of considering people's need to feel comfortable, because humankind needs the spirit, and the victory of the spirit will not be achieved in the comfortable ways that are often taken today. For today the acceptance of the knowledge of initiation is fought with strange weapons.

It was recently a great satisfaction to me when our dear friend Dr. Stein† wrote to Dornach of how he had unhesitatingly put in his place an enemy of the human spiritual life here in the neighborhood. It was on an occasion that is quite significant indeed from a cultural-historical aspect. For there it happened—and you will correct me if I am mistaken, since I was not there myself—when one of our friends cited some saying from the Bible, the minister who was chairing the meeting did not like the truth of those sayings and maintained that here Christ was mistaken. Was that said? [Agreement from the audience.] When today someone does not know how to help themselves in these matters, then that person becomes infallible, but Christ is mistaken. We have come a long way!

You see, all these things testify to the character of the truth of what is living as spiritual life through humanity today. The spiritual life can no longer remain in the sphere of truth when it has become entirely abstract. But one must perceive what is really happening here. The periodical[†] *The Threefold Social Organism* recently gave an account of a meeting that was reported to have taken place here in Stuttgart, at which both Roman Catholics and Protestants took issue with what is disseminated here as spiritual knowledge. The Domkapitular was supposed to have said that a discussion was unnecessary, because people could inform themselves about Rudolf Steiner's teachings from the opposing publications. But the writings of Dr. Steiner were not to be read, because the Pope had forbidden it. In fact this is the latest instruction from the Jesuits of the Congregation of the Holy See that applies primarily to Catholics: that Catholics are forbidden to read writings about Anthroposophy. Therefore today Roman Catholics are required to inform them-selves about what I teach from the writings of the opponents, from the writings of Seiling[†] and some others, because my writings are forbidden by the Holy See. Against this—if one knows the whole attitude of the Roman Catholic Church, and knows how the indi-vidual, integrated the way he or she is, is only a representative of the whole organization—one must raise in all seriousness the question in one's deepest soul: how can such a proceeding be in any way at all reconciled with human morality? Is it not deeply unethical? Today we must not hesitate to ask such questions. We now live in a very serious time, and cannot afford to continue sleeping on in an easy, comfortable, and lazy way. We must without reservation really bring those things that can bring about healing to expression, while at the same time throwing the necessary light on the immorality of the untruthfulness of the present time. And when you come right down to it, this untruthfulness has been spread to no small extent.

Recently Dr. Boos[†] brought me an essay by a doctor of sociology. It began approximately with the following words: What a way it is from the clear thoughts of Waxweiler[†] to the obscure thoughts of Rudolf Steiner! But (the author continues) this gentleman was also the intimate of Wilhelm II,[†] and it is said that just in the last years he stood by Wilhelm II with important counsels, so that one can call him the Rasputin[†] of Wilhelm II. "We do not want to be the one to spread this rumor," it says in the following sentence.

There you can learn two things: first the moral degradation of such a person who makes himself the bearer of this rumor, and his wonderful logic when he says that in spreading this rumor before his readers, he is not the spreader of this rumor. Many people think like this today; abandoned by all the spirits of reality, what they say is already far beyond any reality. For I cannot say: I say something in that I don't say it. For Monsieur Ferrière, who wrote this, creates that kind of a model of the human being. One cannot have anything to do with such morally depraved individuals. I could only determine (and I hope it will be thrown in his face) that I had the following connections with Wilhelm II: first, I once sat in a theater in Berlin, perhaps in the year 1897, upstairs in the first row, and in the middle of the theater Wilhelm II sat in the royal box, and I saw him at a distance of about from here to the end of this hall. The second time I saw him was when he walked behind the coffin of the Grand Duchess of Weimar, quite a long way off. The third time was in the Friedrichstrasse in Berlin, when he rode through the streets with his retinue, his marshal's staff in his hand, and the people were shouting, "Hurrah!" These were all my connections to Wilhelm II; I have not had, or sought any others. In this way today assertions are made, and some of what you read—fixed on the paper with black printer's ink—is not worth any more than this dirty rumor, which is used today to make a heresy of Anthroposophy in the Catholic countries. Today one must go to the source of things; today it is not enough just to accept the things that are said, but it is necessary that people accustom themselves to going to the source of what is said and asserted. But the capacity to recognize the true origin of the outer factual world will only come to bloom for humanity out of a deepening into real spiritual knowledge.

Lecture 2

W HEN in the last few years I spoke at a seasonal festival—Christmas, Easter or Whitsun—I had to point out that, especially on such occasions, we have no right at the present time to celebrate such festivals in the usual way. We cannot forget, so to speak, all the pain and suffering of today, and on such days only remember the greatest things that have played a part in the human development. Especially because of our spiritual point of view of the world, we have the duty to allow all the manifestations of the decline taking hold of humanity in today's culture. We must allow all this to stream in, even right up to the Christmas tree. Today we truly have the duty to take up the birth of Christ Jesus into our hearts and souls in a way that does not ignore the frightful decline that has taken hold of the so-called cultured people.

For particularly on this day it is up to us to bring up the question: Has even the thought of Christmas been subjected to the universal forces of decline?

Do we still feel, when we speak about Christmas today, what human beings should feel when they direct their thoughts and feelings to this festival of Christ? Does humanity in general have a feeling for the real purpose of the part played by the whole Mystery of Golgotha in human development? Today we light up our Christmas trees, we speak in old customary phrases and words about the things connected with the Christmas festival. But all too often we avoid fully awakening our consciousness to the necessity of saying: a decline is at hand—where are you, power of Christ, to really help us so that we can bring about a new uprising? For that much should have become clear to you from our discussions over recent decades concerning the spiritual view of the world, that only with the help of the power of Christ will it be possible to imbue decadent culture with the impulse that will enable it to rise up once again.

In these days one must often think of people who, in the middle and last third of the nineteenth century, despite a certain materialistic frame of mind, certainly spoke with more honesty than the majority do today. Today I want to remind you of a rather materialistically minded personality, the Swabian David Friedrich Strauss.[†] As you know, *The Old and the New Faith* by David Friedrich Strauss is in a certain way a bible of materialism. Among the questions he poses in this book is: can we still be Christians? David Friedrich Strauss gives an answer, which has the peculiar characteristic of being born out of an "ur"-materialistic mindset, but is honest at the same time. David Friedrich Strauss develops the idea of a world structure that is only built up out of material physical laws, where the human being also contains nothing besides physical laws. And from this conviction he answers the question of whether we can still be Christians with an honest "no."

The people who represent this natural scientific view of the world, as David Friedrich Strauss does out of the consciousness of this age, cannot be Christians. Thus out of the "no" of David Friedrich Strauss there speaks a fatal, but altogether honest state of mind, and today one sometimes has the feeling that if only the so-called official representatives of this or the other religious creed could be as honest as David Friedrich Strauss! If only they could realize that even though they use the name of Christ, fundamentally they are working against Christianity!

Nowadays we may not conveniently close our eyes to the most essential and important developments of the time. Some may not think it to be in the spirit of Christmas (I do think it is) if I mention an experience I had in connection with a spiritual investigation of something immediate and actual at this present time.

You know those people, particularly in Central Europe, who are largely to blame—as much as people may be blamed for such things—for the dreadful circumstances we experience today [World War I]. What did they do after Europe was struck by disaster? They write books! And so we have books from the greatest variety of people. We have a Tirpitz book,[†] we have a Ludendorff book,[†] and I could still name several others, but I restrict myself to these two. You see, with the help of spiritual knowledge one can do the following experiment. We can, entirely within the sense of a spiritual-scientific outlook, put the question to ourselves: what form of thinking is expressed in the books of Tirpitz, Ludendorff, and their like? I have tried to examine this question from all sides in a conscientious way, and have asked myself: what kind of thought forms do these men have, on whom depends so much of the destiny of Europe? But if we do not proceed in an abstract way, but penetrate concretely into such things, then we must make comparisons, and so I asked myself: when perhaps were such thought forms cultivated in the normal course of European development such as Tirpitz and Ludendorff are now doing? And after a conscientious examination of the facts it turns out that at about the time of the Roman Caesar, people thought in this way. Basically there is no difference between the way Julius Caesar thought and lived in his soul—let us say in his Gallic wars—and the way Tirpitz and Ludendorff now formulate their thoughts. But that means that these people have a thought life that is completely untouched by Christendom, for Julius Caesar lived before the Mystery of Golgotha took place. And all that these people say, when from time to time the name of Christ Jesus crosses their lips, is nothing but a vain lie, because their soul life has developed in such a way that they have nothing to do with actual Christendom.

From many considerations we of course know that when something develops at the right time, then fundamentally it is good for humanity. It is something else if it remains stuck and then appears later on; when that is the case, such as when what was appropriate at Caesar's time still plays a role in the twentieth century, then it becomes something Luciferic. For if something remains active that really belonged to another time, it becomes Luciferic; that indeed is the essence of what is Luciferic.

And now we ask once more: how can it come about that those personalities that destiny has raised up to take on positions of leadership have remained behind in this way? If we want to answer this question we must observe those who pretend to penetrate their spiritual life with the Christ impulse, but who actually work in an anti-Christian sense. We must direct our attention to many official representatives of religious denominations, who supposedly quote from the Gospels, but who oppose everything that really wants to be said about the living Christ in our time. The most anti-Christian people are today frequently found among the priests, the preachers of the so-called Christian denominations. Whoever investigates this kind of thing among all the publications, such as the book by Adolf Harnack,[†] *Das Wesen des Christentums* (The nature of Christianity), considered by many to establish the tone in these matters, will receive the answer to such a question. If in this book one crosses out the name of Christ and replaces it with the name of some general, unknown god who rules and weaves through nature just as he does in the life of the human being, if one crosses out the name of Christ and puts in its place the Old Testament name of Yahweh, then the book becomes more true that it now is, because only then does it make sense. The fact is evident that Harnack knows nothing of the real being of Christ, that he venerates a general, indeterminate god and then attaches the name of Christ to it. And who is this Adolf Harnack? He is the theologian who set the tone for the spiritual direction out of which sprang up the likes of Tirpitz and Ludendorff! Because no real revelation of Christ came anymore from the representatives of the denominations, there is no perception of the real Christ revelation by the people who are connected with current events. When they speak of the Christmas festival, it has no meaning whatever for the thousands and millions of people of today, for they do not know the being of Christ Jesus in the way one needs to know him in our present time.

We must look at such things if we want to become clear in a deeper sense about the reasons for the downward trend in what is happening today and in human life under these circumstances.

I have often spoken to you here[†] about that important event that took place in the last third of the nineteenth century, through which a special relationship was established between what we call the archangelic power of Michael and the destiny of humankind. I have drawn your attention to the fact that since November of 1879, Michael must be the regent, so to speak, for all those who want to bring to humanity the right powers for its healthy progress.

In our time, when we say something like this, we point out two things: an objective fact, and how that objective fact is related to all that human beings want to engage in their will and in their consciousness. The objective fact is simply that in November 1879, beyond the sphere of the physical world, in the supersensible, the following took place: Michael won the power for himself, that when human beings come towards him with all that lives in their souls, he can so penetrate them with his strength that they can transform the old materialistic power of comprehension (which until then had become so great in humanity) into a spiritual power of comprehension. That is the objective fact; it has taken place. We can say of it: Michael has entered into a different relationship with humanity since November 1879 than he had previously. But it is necessary that we serve Michael. What I mean by that will be best clarified if I explain the following.

You know that, before the Mystery of Golgotha took place on the Earth, the Hebrews of the Old Testament looked up to their Yahweh or Jehovah. Those of the Hebrew priests who perceived Yahweh with full consciousness knew that they could not approach Yahweh directly with human knowledge. Even the name was considered unpronounceable, and when it had to be spoken of only a sign was made that is similar to certain sign relationships we search for in eurythmy. But it was clear to these priests that the human being could approach Yahweh through Michael. They called Michael the Countenance of Yahweh. Just as we come to know human beings when we look into their visage, when we reach a conclusion from the mildness of their visage about the mildness of their soul, and about their character from the way they look at us—in the same way the Old Testament priests wanted to reach conclusions about Yahweh, whom it was not possible for humanity to reach, based on what crept into their soul as atavistic clairvoyant visions of the visages of

Yahweh and Michael in their dreams. These priests had the correct attitude towards Michael and Yahweh; they had the right attitude to Michael because they knew that when the human beings of that time turned to Michael, they would find the strength of Yahweh through Michael, which was fitting for the human being of that time to seek.

Since then other rulers of the soul of humanity have stood in the place of Michael; but since November of 1879, Michael has appeared once again and can be made active in the life of the human soul if one seeks the way to him. And today, these ways are the ways of spiritual-scientific knowledge. One could equally well say the "Michael Ways" as "the ways of spiritual-scientific knowledge." But just since that time when Michael entered into a relationship with human souls in this way to once again become their direct inspirer through three centuries, the demonic counterforces have also set to work most powerfully, having previously prepared themselves. So a call went out through the world that now passes through the hearts and minds of the people, which during our so-called war years (actually years of terror) has become a great misapprehension in the world.

What then would have become of the Hebrew people of the Old Testament, if they had wanted to approach Yahweh directly, instead of coming close to him through Michael? They would have become intolerant and egotistical as a people, a people only able to think of themselves. For Yahweh is the god connected to everything natural, and who expresses his being in the connection between the generations of the people and in their character as a people. Only because at that time the old Hebrew people wanted to approach Yahweh through Michael did they save themselves from becoming so egotistical that not even Christ Jesus could have come forth out of their midst. Because they penetrated themselves with the strength of Michael, as that strength then was, the Hebrew people thereby did not impregnate themselves with forces producing such a strong folk-egoism as would have resulted from a direct approach to Yahweh.

Now today Michael is the world regent once again, but humanity is required to relate to him in a new way—because now Michael is not the countenance of Yahweh, but the countenance of Christ Jesus. Now we should approach Christ through Michael. But for the most part humanity has not yet struggled through to that realization; humanity has atavistically preserved the old qualities of perception through which one approached Michael when he was still the mediator for Yahweh. And so today humanity still has a wrong relationship to Michael, which shows itself in a characteristic way.

Again and again during the war years one heard the great falsehood: independence for each, and even the very smallest nation. This sentiment is a false one, because in this time of Michael it is human individuals, not groups of people, that are important. This falsehood is nothing but an effort to penetrate every single group of people with the pre-Christian Michael strength of the Old Testament. As paradoxical as it may sound, there exists today among so-called civilized humanity the tendency to transform Luciferically what was justified in the Hebrews of the Old Testament into the innermost impulse of every group of people. Today, with a pre-Christian state of mind, one wants to create Polish nations, American nations, French nations, and so forth. We strive to follow Michael in the way that was appropriate before the Mystery of Golgotha, when through him one should find Yahweh, a god of the people. Today, through him we should find Christ Jesus, the divine leader of all humankind. We must find feelings and ideas that have nothing to do with any human differences on the Earth; but these we cannot seek on the surface, but must seek them where the human soul and spirit is pulsating, by way of spiritual science. We must decide to seek the real Christ by way of spiritual science, in other words in a Michaelic way—the Christ who can only be sought and found on the basis of a spiritual striving for the truth. Otherwise we should rather put out all the Christmas lights, kill all the Christmas trees, and at least honestly admit to ourselves that we do not want to have any recollection of what Christ Jesus brought into the development of humankind.

And so there resounds to us out of the memoirs of people of today a pre-Christian (which in our time means anti-Christian) state of mind. When people we consider as representative make themselves heard, such as Wilson, then in those Fourteen Points[†] he gave resounds an entirely Old Testament state of mind, which in our time becomes a Luciferic state of mind. Where does this come from? What is going on here?

If we go back in time to the development of humanity before the Mystery of Golgotha, in ancient times when Eastern culture was developing, we find on the Earth a human personality within the culture that later became the Chinese culture of today. This personality was the human incarnation of Lucifer, who at that time really walked upon the Earth, and who was the bearer of the human light that was the basis of pre-Christian wisdom, except that of the Hebrew people. What emanated from the Lucifer incarnation thousands of years before the Mystery of Golgotha still streamed through what lived in the Greek civilization in the arts, in their view of the world, and in statesmanship.

We must in particular be clear about the fact that everything we today call human understanding is still a gift of that Lucifer, so long as we have not spiritualized it. Only we must not develop the pedantic, bourgeois, sectarian attitude: Luciferic—that is something dreadful, that must be stripped away. If one wants to strip it away, one takes it in all the more, because over thousands of years of human development it has become necessary to accept the heritage of the incarnated Lucifer. Then came the Mystery of Golgotha.

But then a time will come when, just as Lucifer once incarnated in the East as an earthly personality in order to prepare the coming of Christianity, the real Ahriman will likewise appear in the West in an earthly incarnation. We are approaching that time when Ahriman will actually wander over the Earth. As truly as Lucifer and Christ actually wandered about as human beings, so Ahriman will wander over the Earth with an intellectual faculty of tremendous power. We human beings do not have the task to prevent the incarnation of Ahriman, but we do have the task of preparing humanity in such a way that a right assessment of Ahriman will be made. For Ahriman will have tasks and will have to do one thing and another, but human beings will have to assess and utilize in the right way what comes into the world through Ahriman. Humanity will only be able to do this if we can today orient ourselves in the right way to what Ahriman is already sending to the Earth from other worlds in order to be able to operate on the Earth without being noticed. Ahriman must not operate on the Earth without being noticed; we must fully recognize his peculiar nature, and be able to face up to him in full consciousness.

Now, while I am lecturing here in Stuttgart, I will show you some of the things that must be carefully watched in the development of humanity until the incarnation of Ahriman, so that when he comes he will be properly evaluated. Today I would only like to draw your attention to one thing: in relation to Ahriman, just as bad as the worst materialistic view of the world are some of the current interpretations of the Gospels. When today the Gospels are simply taken as they are by the representatives of the so-called religious communities, and when every new revelation is rejected, then such a devotion to the Gospels, such a way to practice Christianity signifies the best way to prepare oneself in an Ahrimanic sense for the earthly appearance of Ahriman. A great number of representatives of the so-called confessions of today are paving the way for Ahriman, in that they disregard the truth, "I am with you always, even until the end of the world,"† in that they declare all that comes forth out of a direct perception of the contemporary Christ to be heretical, in that they conveniently hold on to the Gospels in a literal way, but literal only according to them. There should be a wisdom to protect people from holding on to the Gospels in this way, since in a purely external way the four Gospels contradict one another when approached only through our intelligence. Whoever today does not advance to a spiritual interpretation of the Gospels spreads a mendacious interpretation of them, because he deludes people about the external contradictions that exist in the Gospels. And to delude people about their most important concerns is just what best advances the aims of Ahriman.

It is very necessary for people of the present time to place Christ in between Ahriman and Lucifer. The strength of Christ must penetrate us. But as human beings we must always seek the balance between what would, so to speak, draw us up in an extravagant, mystical way and what wants to drag us down to the Earth in a materialistically intellectual and heavy, pedantic way. At every moment we must seek the balance between what would uplift us Luciferically, and what would make us want to strive downward in an Ahrimanic way—in the search for this balance lies the Christ. And only when we strive to find this balance, can we find the Christ.

Due to an unusual circumstance, something very remarkable happened in humanity's more recent development, in the time when materialism was entering in. I will only refer to two documents: Milton's *Paradise Lost*† and Klopstock's *Messiah*.† There the spiritual worlds are described as if a paradise had been lost and the human being had been thrown out of it. Both Milton's *Paradise Lost* and Klopstock's *Messiah* deal with a duality in the world, with the contrast of good and evil, the divine and the diabolical. But you see, that is the great error of recent times, that one pictures the culture of the world as a duality, while it must be pictured as a trinity. There are the upward-striving Luciferic forces living in the human blood that both approach the human being in what is mystical, extravagant, and full of fantasy and degenerate into the fantastical. Then there are the Ahrimanic forces that live in everything that is dried up and heavy, physiologically speaking, in the bony system, and in the middle between the two stands the Christian element. The first is Luciferic, the second Ahrimanic, and in the middle between the two is what is Christian.

What has happened in recent times? Something that humanity should observe with truly spiritual-intellectual fervor, because if we do not understand this we will not find our way to Christmas in the right way. How do we read Milton and Klopstock and their descriptions of the supersensible world today? We read them in such a way that Luciferic characteristics are carried over into everything we want to call divine. Such men as Milton and Klopstock want to describe the battle between the Luciferic, which to them appears as the divine, and the Ahrimanic. And a great part of what present-day humanity describes as divine is merely Luciferic. But we do not rightly recognize it, just as little as we do the Ahrimanic. This still plays into Goethe's *Faust*, when we find the "Lord" confronted by Mephistopheles—for even Goethe could still not separate the Ahrimanic from the Luciferic. Thus his Mephistopheles became an intermingling of Lucifer and Ahriman. I have already referred to this in my booklet *Goethe's Spiritual Nature.*[†] Today one is a Goetheanist in the true sense not if, as some academics and others of the present day do, one simply quotes Goethe verbatim, but when one also sees what had to change in Goethe, particularly when one follows his view of the world beyond the year 1832. But the way must be found to quietly admit to ourselves that much of the Luciferic element was contained in what was called the divine during the materialistic centuries, and that we can take much of what people use to spread as religion as merely words that enter humanity on Luciferic wings. Only then, when people will again recognize the duality of the Luciferic, which wants to lead them upwards, and the Ahrimanic that wants to lead them below themselves, and come to recognize what is truly Christian, will people once again stand before the Christmas event in its true meaning. Through the true meaning of Christmas we can remember how what actually gives real meaning to the Earth entered into the development of humanity.

Today one should sometimes think of Leonardo da Vinci.[†] Leonardo once painted his great picture, the Last Supper with Christ surrounded by his apostles. He painted a long time on this picture: twenty years. He wanted to paint a great deal into this picture. He could not finish because he tried again and again to paint the figure of Judas in the right way. Now according to the city government of Milan, the abbot of the monastery for which the picture was being painted was his immediate superior. When a new abbot was named, he was not as easygoing as the old one, but critical, giving Leonardo a hard time and demanding of him that the picture should now be finally completed. Leonardo replied that now he could indeed finish it, for the new abbot had provided him with a model for Judas. Then he shortly painted the face of Judas that we see in the picture. Just as the way the face of Judas appeared to Leonardo at the beginning of a new time in our history, so today we already have ample reason to really inscribe into our hearts and souls how he, whose birth we are commemorating at this holy festival of Christmas, is betrayed most of all by many of those who declare that they prepare his feasts based on their convictions. We know that this Christmas festival also belongs to what later arose out of the development of Christianity. It was only in the third and fourth centuries that people began to celebrate the birth of Christ in these December days. Some centuries had already elapsed since the event of Golgotha when the perception of that event allowed something new to arise, even as radically new as the institution of the Christmas festival at that time. And much, much later it was still possible to plant new things into Christianity. Also then one had to fight against many of those who called themselves true Christians. But today there are many people at work who don't want to be found wrong (as their own convictions were found to be wrong when the Christmas festival was instituted in the third and fourth centuries), who rigidly cling only to what they say is written, rejecting every life-containing revelation. Today it is quite dreadful with those who are half asleep, who with their immoral attitude often besmirch what wants to enter into the spiritual life—but most dreadful are those who out of conviction betray even the actual spirit of Christian development.

That is the serious mood into which the lights of the Christmas tree want to transport us today. I wanted to point out these things today, but it is out of a different context that I will speak to you the next time.

Lecture 3

STUTTGART, DECEMBER 28, 1919

Fʀᴏᴍ the discussions we have had here for some time, especially from those of recent days, it should be apparent how very necessary it is that the knowledge of initiation should enter into human cultural development. Today we must already say entirely without reservation: the rescue of humanity from a downward course of development depends literally on making humanity aware of the revelation that can only be experienced through spiritual cognition.

Emotional or logical objections may be made from one side or another—it may be said that in our time it will be difficult for large numbers of people to accept knowledge that for now can only come from the few individuals who have developed the capacity of looking into the spiritual world to a high degree. But even seemingly justifiable objections say absolutely nothing against the fact, which speaks loud and clear, that without the acceptance of what we call Anthroposophically oriented spiritual science, the culture of humanity must sink into the abyss and the work on Earth must fall to powers that will not include humanity in their further development in the world. Things will not go otherwise unless enough people fill themselves with what I have just tried to say, and healing in this direction can be brought to humanity. For only those who absolutely will not look at what is happening in the world as a result of these last catastrophic years can close their eyes to the fact that we are starting out on the road to ruin, and that only something new can lead us away from this path. Whatever one may look for within this destructive process itself, it can never become anything else but a force of destruction. Now only what will really draw on sources that have not belonged to the Earth's development up till now can bring about a force for reconstruction.

But there are significant difficulties standing in the way of obtaining results from such sources. It is often said that the science of initiation could not without reservation be brought to humanity, because a particular kind of reception is necessary for it. You see, again and again people listen to this, but again and again this is also just what is always being sinned against. Let us take only a very simple example: one of the very first, most elementary requirements for receiving the science of initiation is that those who receive it must try to overcome what for example could be called a desire to be looked up to, in particular when they express a judgment comparing their own personality with that of other people. Now it is quite easy to see that just in what we call the Anthroposophical Society—what would be the point of not saying it?—it is admitted over and over again that this is right; but we see that just the most disagreeable things exist within a movement such as the Anthroposophical one, that just in it opposing intrigues and mutual envy take root.

I will only just point out these manifestations. For today I must speak of the other, even greater difficulties facing the introduction of initiation science into the culture of the Earth.

You see, to begin with, what has to be shown to humanity in a comprehensive way is what one could call the mystery of the human will. This mystery has been hidden from the culture of humanity in recent times, especially since the middle of the fifteenth century, since the beginning of the fifth post-Atlantean epoch. One can say the worldview of recent humanity knows almost nothing about the will. We have often characterized it:[†] the human individual never experiences the actual nature of the will during waking consciousness. Awake, human beings experience the nature of their conceptions, in dreaming the nature of their feelings, but even when awake they are partly asleep with regard to the will. We go through the world as so-called awake human beings, but are only awake to our conceptions, half awake, dreaming in our feelings, and are completely asleep to the will. Let us not deceive ourselves about this. We have conceptions about our willing, but only when the will becomes a conception, only when the will is portrayed to the intelligence do we experience it when awake.

What is going on there in the depths of the human being, even when we only raise a hand, which means setting our will into motion—of that the normal person of today knows nothing at all. This means that the mystery of the will is completely unknown to human beings of today, and this is really connected with the fact that our whole recent culture, especially what has developed since the fifteenth century, is a culture of the mind, because the culture of natural science is a culture of the mind. In everything that we grasp with the intellect, that we pursue with the mind, the will has the least part to play. Whenever we think, when we imagine, the will of course also plays a part in our imagining, but in a very, very refined way. We are unaware of the pulsation of the will in our imagining, or how else the will functions in our being. In a certain way it is due to the exclusively intellectual culture of recent times that the mystery of the will is completely hidden from the people of this time. If one now approaches the investigation of the will with those means of spiritual science that I have often spoken of here—that is to say, if one tries to enliven, with the help of imagination and inspiration, those forces that can see into the workings that become active when the human being wills—then one realizes that in our physical life between birth and death the will is essentially connected not with the upbuilding processes, but with those of disintegration. If in our brain only upbuilding processes were at work[†]—if only, for example, what is done by the nourishment taken up by the life forces were at work—then we would not be able to develop a soul and spiritual life through the instrument of our nerves and brain. It is only because of the continual process of breaking down or disintegration in our brain that the soul and spiritual element can secure a place in what is disintegrating. But that is just where the will is at work. The will of the human being is essentially something that during our physical life is already partly working for our death. Regarding our head organization, we are constantly dying; every moment we are dying. We only live because the rest of our organization works against this constant dying of the head. But it is the will above all else that is active in this dying of the head. In our head continually takes place what, apart from ourselves, is objectively happening in the world outside when we have passed through physical death.

Our corpse really is of no concern to us, to the extent that we are human individualities and are entering the soul-spiritual worlds through the gate of death, but it is of great concern to the universe, because this corpse is delivered in some form to the elements of the Earth—through cremation or burial, it does not really matter how. There, in its own way, it continues to do what our human will partially does in our nerve system, our sensory system, during the life between birth and death. We can imagine and think due to our will destroying something in us. We give our corpse over to the Earth, and with the help of this disintegrating corpse, which merely continues the same process that we were partially carrying out during our life, the whole Earth imagines and thinks, so to speak. What goes on continuously in the Earth through the reciprocal activity between the Earth and the dead corpses (I once characterized this to you from other points of view some months ago) is an activity that is quite similar in character to the will activity continually at work unconsciously in our nerve and sensory system in breaking down, disintegrating, and working towards a corpse-like condition between birth and death. It is the same will that between birth and death works by means of disintegration by connecting itself with our "I," that same will within the boundaries of our skin that after our death works cosmically through our corpse in the thinking and imagination of the whole Earth. Thus we are cosmically connected with what one can call the soul-spiritual process of the whole of Earth's existence. This concept is of great weight, for it concretely places the human being in the cosmic aspect of our Earth existence. This demonstrates how related the human will is to what the forces of death are doing in our Earth existence; it shows the relationship of the human will to the working of the general world will in disintegration and in bringing about the conditions for death on the Earth.

But just as our continuing development in the spiritual world after we die depends on not having a physical body anymore—on

not working with bodily forces, but with other ones—so does
a thriving, further development of the whole Earth depend on
whether humanity unites itself not with these death forces, but with
life forces that develop themselves in a different direction than these
death forces. To say this before humanity of today, so filled with
personal intentions and feelings, is already something rather severe,
because the seriousness of such a truth is felt today only to a very
limited degree. Humanity has indeed forgotten how to take great
truths with the necessary deep seriousness. But despite that, it must
further be asked: how then is what lies in the human will, as I have
described it, actually connected with the disintegration processes in
outer nature? It is here, we might say, where the greatest illusion
confronts the human being of today. What does a human being
actually do when looking at nature? Yes, there is a natural process
taking place. Before, another process took place that is its cause;
before that again another one, and so on. In this way modern people
find a chain of causes and effects in nature, and are very proud of it
when they comprehend the outer world by following the thread of
causality. What comes about from this? Well, ask any conscientious
geologist, physicist, chemist, or any other orthodox natural scientist
(though they may often shy away from drawing the ultimate conclusions based on their view of the world) whether they do not have
to imagine that the Earth—the stones, plants, and many animals
too—would have developed just as they have if the human being
had not been there, if no houses, no machines, no airships had been
built by the buffaloes, bulls, and so on. Everything else that today
we do not consider the work of human beings would all have been
there from beginning to end, even if the human beings had not
been there, because in outer nature there exists a chain of causes and
effects. What came later is the result of what came before, and actually the human being was not there at the formation of this chain of
events, according to present-day opinion! This view contains exactly
the same error as the following: imagine that I write a sentence on
the blackboard: "Stuttgart is a city." Now somebody comes across
this sentence and says that they will scientifically investigate what
they find written on this blackboard. Starting from the back, we first

find a letter *y*. This comes out of the *t*. Then the *t* comes out of the preceding *i*, the *i* out of the preceding *c*, and so on. Each time we have the effect of the preceding cause. The y is the effect of the *t*, the *t* is the effect of the *i*, and so forth. You see, it is nonsense. Each letter only exists because I have written it, and the preceding letter did not of course create the subsequent one. A thorough, unprejudiced examination of the character of the processes in nature will convince us of the same. We say, under the great illusion of contemporary science: effects are the result of their causes. It is not so. In nature we must look for the actual causes elsewhere, just as we must look for the cause for the sequence of letters in our understanding. And where, by and large, lie the causes for what happens in nature? Only through spiritual perception can we determine that the causes lie with humanity. Do you know where you must look if you want to see the real causes for the development of nature on the Earth? You must investigate how the will, deeply asleep in our present state of consciousness, is located in the center of gravity of the human being—that is, in the abdomen. Only a portion of the will is active in the human head, and the greater part of it is centered in the rest of the organism. What comes into existence as the outer development of nature depends on what the human being is in relation to this unconscious will. Up to now we could only quote one significant case in this development, but it applies to the whole of it.

I have often drawn your attention to the fact that during the time of Atlantis, people devoted themselves to a kind of black magic. As a result the ice age spread over the civilized world. But in a most comprehensive sense everything in the development of nature is in reality the result of the will activity not of a single human being, but of the working together of various will forces coming from the human centers of gravity. If a sufficiently developed being were to study the Earth, let us say from Mars or Mercury, in order to understand how the development of nature takes place here, then this being would not describe nature as would a person who wants to seem educated. Such a being would look over the Earth and say: "Down there on the Earth are many points where the forces that bring about the development of nature are centered." But for this being these points would not lie outside in nature, but always inside the human beings. Someone looking from outside would feel they must look at what is within humanity if they want to seek the causes for what happens in the development of nature. This insight into the relationship of human will activity with the overall development of nature will have to become an integral part of the future natural science of humanity. Of course we can be deceived if we only observe the development of nature as far as the end of our nose—then of course the relationship will not be apparent. With such a natural science, human beings will feel themselves responsible for what they are in quite a different way than they generally feel today. From being a citizen of the Earth, human beings will become cosmic citizens. They will learn to regard themselves as belonging to the cosmos.

But consider that just as soon as one draws attention to such things, the knowledge of them becomes part of us. This knowledge is not like the shadow of our intellectual knowledge, but is derived much more from the reality of things and therefore it works in a way that is much more real.

And since it works in a more real way than the shadow-like knowledge of present-day humanity, it is then necessary that human beings take seriously what is revealed through this knowledge. One cannot remain a citizen of the cosmos in the sense just described on the one hand, and on the other still remain the old kind of pedant that the last few centuries since the middle of the fifteenth century have produced in the humanity of today. One cannot on the one hand want to become a participant in cosmic events, and on the other hand indulge in frequent gossip sessions about our fellow human beings, as has been happening in the bourgeois times since the middle of the fifteenth century. It is necessary that another ethos, other moral impulses, find their way throughout humanity, if at the same time the science of initiation is to enter in a serious way. For today a special hindrance to the entry of this initiation science is everything that is unrighteously preparing for the appearance of Ahriman on our Earth. I have just recently referred to this fact, in order to characterize a little for you the right festival mood for this year's Christmas; I will now briefly recapitulate.

When we go back in the history of the Earth, then we find before our present materialistic culture the Greco-Roman culture going back to the eighth century B.C.E. We see appearing a few centuries after the beginning of this Greco-Roman period what we might call the old life of wisdom of ancient times, at that time already filtered in the land of Greece. Nietzsche had strange, even morbid feelings in this connection. From the beginning of his intellectual work he felt himself to be an opponent of Socrates,[†] and he never tired to speak again and again of the greater worth of the pre-Socratic Greek culture as compared with the Socratic and post-Socratic. I will not enter into this matter further, other than to say to you: it is certainly true that on the one hand a great epoch of humanity began with Socrates, one that found its culmination in the transition of the fourteenth and fifteenth centuries. But for this age of Socrates time has now run out, really run out. The Socratic epoch took from the prior impulsive wisdom merely the logic, the dialectic. This taking of only the logic from the old clairvoyant wisdom is the characteristic of our Western culture. It has also left its stamp on Christianity, because the theology of the West is also a dialectical one. But what comes up in Greece as dialectic, as spirituality filtered to abstraction, goes back to the Mysteries of the East; and with these mysteries were also those that founded the culture that later became the Chinese culture within which Lucifer incarnated. This should not be concealed, that Lucifer himself was once in a body, just as the Christ wandered about the Earth in a body at the time of the Mystery of Golgotha. But one pedantically misunderstands this Luciferic incarnation, when one wants to regard everything that came out of Lucifer as a kind of touch-me-not.

From Lucifer, for example, the height of Greek culture itself came about, the real art of that time, and humanity's impulse for art the way we actually still think about it.

But in Europe all of that has become frozen into phrases and devoid of content. And it was through Luciferic wisdom that Christianity first became understood in Europe. That is what is significant—that in Greek wisdom, which developed as a gnosis to understand the Mystery of Golgotha, the old Luciferic wisdom was also at work and gave form to the ancient gnosis. At that time it was Christianity's greatest victory that the Mystery of Golgotha clothed itself in what Lucifer gave to the world. But while the culture of Lucifer, which was given to humanity through his actual incarnation, was ebbing away, the tide was gradually rising for what was preparing for the future incarnation of Ahriman on the Earth. When the time is ripe (and it is preparing itself for that) Ahriman will incarnate in the West in a human body. This event must take place, just as Lucifer and Christ had to incarnate. This fact is prescribed for the development of the Earth. What is important is only this: to face up to the fact as to properly prepare for it; for Ahriman will not wait to act until he appears on the Earth as a human being, but he is already preparing in the supersensible worlds for his appearance. He is already working into the development of humanity, and from where he is now he seeks the tools to prepare himself for what is to come.

Now, an essential way to achieve a favorable effect of what Ahriman is to bring to humanity—he will bring positive things, the same as Lucifer—is that humanity has the right attitude to it. It all depends on humanity not sleeping through his appearance. When the incarnated Ahriman appears in the West, the birth record will say John William Smith is born (of course that won't be his name), and people will look upon him as a good citizen just like other citizens, and they will be unaware of what is actually happening. Our university professors will quite certainly not take care that we are awake for this. For them, what will appear there will be John William Smith. But what is important is that in this Ahrimanic age people know that only outwardly will we be dealing with John William Smith, and that inwardly Ahriman is present. We cannot let ourselves be deceived and sleepily deluded by what is going on. Yes, already now we must not be under any illusion that these things are being prepared. Among the most important means that Ahriman has to work down from the other world is this: to promote the abstract thinking of humanity. And because this abstract thinking is so popular these days, people are well paving the way for the appearance of Ahriman in ways favorable to him. For Ahriman to trap the whole Earth into his own development, nothing could better prepare than pursuing this life of abstraction, which today has even penetrated the social life. That is one of the feints, one of the tricks, whereby Ahriman thinks to prepare for his mastery of the Earth. Instead of showing people from actual experience what should be done, they are told about general theories, about social theories. Those who talk about theories find what comes just from experience to be abstract, because they haven't the least notion about real life. All of this is the Ahrimanic way of preparation.

But there is still another way of preparing for Ahriman (this is also something that people today now need to know about), which can happen through an erroneous conception of the Gospels. Of course you know there are numerous people today, especially among the official representatives of one or other of the denominations, who are fighting tooth and nail just against what is coming out from the science of initiation to give us a new understanding of Christ. Such people, if they don't only do homage to rationalism, still accept the Gospels; but what do they know about the actual nature of the Gospels? People of this kind were just the ones who applied the outer, worldly, historic-scientific method to the Gospels in the nineteenth century. And what happened to these Gospels using the scientific method of the nineteenth century? Nothing, except that this conception of the Gospels gradually became materialized. The first thing that was noted was the contradictions contained in the four Gospels. And then, from the perception of these contradictions, a downward slide took place to what I call "Schmiedelei." For in the end, what is all that comes out of the Gospel research of Schmiedel from Basel? I mean the theologian Professor Schmiedel, not our Dr. Schmiedel.[†] What is this, I would like to say, other than taking the Gospels off their hinges? What is dear old Schmiedel looking for in the Gospels? He is seeking to prove that they are not just products of fantasy, only intended to glorify Christ Jesus, and arrives at a limited number of points—Schmeidel's famous main points—in which unfavorable things were also said about the Christ. These, he thinks, would have been left out if the Gospels had only been written for the glorification of Jesus. So one finally has the feeling that he enters into everything where Christ Jesus is portrayed in a negative light, in order to salvage a tiny bit of conventional knowledge for the Gospels. But even this tiny bit will fall away; nothing will be won from conventional knowledge that will be able to prove the authenticity of the Gospels in the way these gentlemen would like. To have the right attitude to these Gospels one would have to know why they came to exist—in other words, one would have to know what they actually want. This we will only come to recognize with minds really fructified by what can emerge from spiritual science.

But if we enter deeply into the Gospels, if we absorb their content and their power, then we come to the point of gaining a soul content from them. No outer knowledge of history will solve their riddles for us, but we can penetrate deeply into them, and then receive a content for the soul. This soul content is a great hallucination, a refined hallucination, to be sure—the hallucination of the Mystery of Golgotha. The greatest thing that can be gained from the Gospels is the hallucination of the Mystery of Golgotha, nothing more and nothing less. You see, this secret is just what is known to the newer Catholic Church. Therefore the Church doesn't want laymen to finally know about the Gospels, because it is afraid they might then realize that one cannot get a historical account of the Christ mystery from the Gospels, but only a hallucination of this Mystery of Golgotha;

I could also call it an imagination, because the hallucination is so refined that it is a real imagination. But it is not possible to gain more than an imagination from the Gospel content itself.

What is the way from the imagination to the reality? The way is opened up, you see, through spiritual science—not through what lies outside spiritual science, but through spiritual science alone. Which means, the imagination of the Gospels must be raised to reality through spiritual science. It is in Ahriman's utmost interest to so prepare his incarnation that human beings do not find the way through spiritual science from the imagination in the Gospels to the reality of the Mystery of Golgotha. Just as Ahriman has the greatest interest to preserve the sense for the abstract, so does he also have the greatest interest that humanity more and more develops the kind of piety that is merely based on the Gospels. If you think about that, you will understand that a great many of the denominations of the present time are paving the way for the realization of Ahriman's purposes on the Earth. How could one better serve Ahriman than if one decided to utilize an available external power in order to command those, who believe in that power and submit to it, that they should not read Anthroposophical literature! One could certainly not do Ahriman a greater service than to bring it about that a number of people do not read Anthroposophical literature. Those people who have decided to go the way of Anthroposophy have to acquaint themselves with it. There are some facts that just cannot be put in any way other than without reservation and in the light of the truth.

It must be realized that the course of world development is moving towards the incarnation of Ahriman, which will be taking place in the not-so-distant future. The course of world development went from Lucifer's incarnation thousands of years ago and passed through the Mystery of Golgotha, whose working still continues. Ahriman's incarnation must stand in the way of this development, so that through opposition the forces embraced by the Christ impulse are strengthened. Through a veiled cult of the Gospels and through abstraction Ahriman will be helped on his way. Due to an inner need for comfort, many people today shut themselves off from these serious matters. Anthroposophists should not do so; they should rather develop an impetus to do as much as possible for the spread of spiritual science in humanity. It is quite wrong when it is constantly believed that one needs to reach an understanding with people like Traub.† It is senseless to believe that one could come to an understanding with such people, because they don't want to. What is important is to enlighten the rest of humanity about these people, so that they can come to an understanding with us—truly it is for that reason that everything has come about. They would only need, without prejudice, to read what is there, to plunge deep into what is there. One must strictly distinguish between the characteristics of those people who do harm to the further development of humanity and the others to whom we must step up and tell them about the wrongdoers. Any attempt to arrive at an understanding with such people is quite pointless and has no meaning, for these people will only incline towards an understanding when they no longer have any followers who give them something to stand on.

Then they are of themselves quite ready to reach an understanding. The primary necessity consists just in enlightening people about them. If only the striving to reach compromises in this connection did not unfortunately often exist just within our own circles—if only there was the courage for the absolute truth in this connection! It is quite unnecessary for us to ever be under the illusion of bringing about an understanding with this or that person who doesn't want an understanding with us at all. Would it be of any help to us? What is necessary for us is to stand up courageously for the truth, as much as we can. And that, it seems to me, arises quite especially out of the conception of what is connected with human development.

Lecture 4

On this evening it always behooves us to think of how past and future are linked together and connected with all of the cosmic life into which the human being is woven. We think of how past and future are intertwined in every part of our lives, because of all our own individual being was able to do and to think during the bygone year, and what it may intend in the year ahead. With our Anthroposophical spiritual science in mind, we should penetrate those thoughts we must have about our actions of the past year and what we intend to do in the coming year with the requisite seriousness and dignity, by seeing them in a higher light through what we can absorb in a spiritual-scientific way through a consideration of the great cosmic events. How does our life actually relate to the past and future? It is like a mirror. Yes, this comparison with a mirror corresponds much more to reality than we might at first imagine. In fact we stand as if in front of a mirror, just when we are striving for a little self-knowledge. What is being reflected in the mirror is the part of the past that we know about. And behind the mirror lies what for now cannot be looked at, no more than you can see what lies behind a mirror when standing in front of it. Perhaps we have to especially raise the question here: what actually is the reflecting coating in our world mirror that allows what is transparent to become a mirror? In a spatial mirror the back of the glass is coated so that our vision cannot penetrate this glass. What then coats that world mirror, which shows us a reflection of the past, but hides the future behind itself for the time being? It is coated, my dear friends, with our own being—coated with our humaness.

We need only consider that with ordinary knowledge we are in fact unable to become clear about what we ourselves are. We cannot look through ourselves; we look through ourselves no more than we can look through a mirror. Much is reflected back to us when we look into ourselves. What we have experienced and learned is reflected, but our own being hides itself, because we can no more look through into our own self than we can look through an actual mirror. Considered overall, and I would like to say in the abstract, we can regard this mirror comparison the way I have now presented it, but in a particular case it does become somewhat modified. Looking back on our life is indeed like a mirror regarding what is reflected by our inmost soul, but we must admit to ourselves that only a part of what we have experienced is reflected there. When you try to look back at your experiences, they are continually being interrupted. You look back at what today brought to you, but not at what was brought by the night before. The experiences of the night are an interruption. And again you look back at yesterday, but not at the night before yesterday, and so forth. There is a continual intervention of the nighttime experiences not included in one's thoughts. We are deceived when we look back and believe we are looking over our whole life: we, so to speak, piece together only what the days contain, and our life's course passes before our soul with constant interruptions.

We can now ask ourselves: are these interruptions in the course of our life necessary? Yes, they are necessary. If we did not have these interruptions in the course of our life, or rather in the retrospect of our life, we would not as human beings become aware of our "I." We would see the course of our life only filled up by the outer world, and the "I"-consciousness would not enter into our life at all. That we perceive and feel our "I" comes from the fact that the course of our life is constantly broken up by interruptions. The humanity of the present stands in a critical time just with regard to this perceiving of the "I" brought about by the interruptions in the continuity of life. When someone of today looks back and experiences their "I" through the retrospective way just described, then this "I" is empty in a certain respect: we only know about our own "I." The people of former epochs knew more. In the way dreams come shimmering out for the individual during the day from experiences during the night, so the atavistic-clairvoyant perceptions only had the form of dreams; what they contained were realities. One can say: the "I" has been emptied of its atavistic-clairvoyant content that supported people of bygone epochs, which penetrated them with the conviction that they had something in common and were connected with something divine. Out of the atavistic-clairvoyant visions arose for human beings what condensed in their life of feelings into a religious perception and veneration of those to whom the religious cult and religious acts of offering were dedicated.

How does the matter stand today? Today the "I" is empty of these atavistic-clairvoyant visions, and when we look back at the "I" it is, so to speak, more or less only a point in our soul life. The content of this "I" is a firm point of support for everyone, but still only a point. But we are also living in a time when the point should once again become a circle, in which the "I" should once again receive a content. Since the last third of the nineteenth century the spirit world has been reaching so mightily into the sense world in order for the "I" to have a content once more; that is why since the 1870s the spiritual world with its revelations wants to enter once again into our physical existence in a new way. And what we want, based on the ground of Anthroposophically oriented spiritual science, is to willingly take up and put into a humanly communicable form what wants to enter in through spiritual revelations from another world, but one which is supporting ours. What is it that wants to enter in? It is nothing less than what, in a certain respect, guarantees the future of humankind. It is, we could say, not a direct look behind the mirror. But it is a guarantee that when humanity hastens toward the future (which means to set out on the way behind the mirror), what we must do in the future can vigorously take place: what all human beings have to accomplish when we have steeled and strengthened our forces through what is revealed to us from the spiritual world in a spiritual-scientific way.

Just as the "I" was filled for the human being of the past with atavistic-clairvoyant content that guaranteed a connection with the divine, so in our time our "I" should fill itself with a new spiritual content received in full consciousness, which once again provides the tie that binds our soul to the soul being of the divine. What remained behind as the last inheritance of the old atavistic clairvoyance is the abstract thinking and abstract knowledge of the people of today. This remained behind as a dilution of the previous atavistic clairvoyance. People of today can have the feeling that this dilution, this logical-dialectical dilution of the old atavistic-clairvoyant nature can no longer be borne in the soul. Then we will experience a longing to receive something new in our "I." But now a start must be made with what has formed the end of the development of humanity from ancient times up to the present.

In those ancient times humanity had clairvoyant revelations and did not understand them; only later did they learn to do so. Today human beings must first understand, must exert their intellect, and when they exert it through what spiritual science offers, then humanity will once again develop towards the clairvoyant perception of the spiritual. However this is something that most people today still prefer to avoid: to apply their sound human understanding to comprehend spiritual science. If one wanted to avoid doing that, then one would also want to avoid allowing spiritual revelations to enter our earthly world altogether.

Thus past and future are linked together on this present New Year's—or Cosmic New Year's Day. It is really a kind of Cosmic New Year, what we have today. The future lies like an enormous question before us—not like a vague, abstract question, but as a concrete question. How do we approach what has wanted to enter our earthly world ever more and more as a question to humanity, even as a spiritual revelation, ever since the last third of the nineteenth century? And how should we relate this to what has been revealed in the past? This would have to be perceived in a living way, and then one would feel what significance it has to give way to one's longing for an Anthroposophically oriented spiritual science. Then one would feel the seriousness and dignity of spiritual-scientific striving. Just at the present time it would be necessary to have this feeling, because we don't really appeal to something arbitrary in the human being, rather to what wants to reveal itself as knowledge of the world out of the development of the world itself—we appeal to what the gods want with humanity, so to speak. But the fact is, that when one turns to the spirit on the one hand, then, on the other, those people who want only to worship what was in the past are drawn towards the spirit of contradiction or opposition. And the more we attempt to take hold of the spirit of what is to be the future of humanity, the more will the people looking to the past be obsessed by the spirit of opposition.

In humanity today it is noticeable how religious feeling is trying to imbue new life into itself. It consists mostly of fumbling attempts. Spiritual-scientific attempts should not be fumbling ones. Through them the real, concrete spirit world should be taken hold of. But, I would like to say, people stand before us as if they had a notion of that and they say: The mere religious tradition is not enough for us, we want to have an inner religious experience. We don't only want to have the information that, according to tradition and reports handed down, Christ lived in Palestine so and so many years ago and that he died—we want to experience the Christ experience in our own souls. In many areas we see such things occurring in people who believe that something of the Christ experience arose in their inmost soul. They are fumbling attempts that are often even questionable, because then the people are right away satisfied in their self-seeking souls and reject any inclination towards the spirit. But they are there, these longings for inner spiritual experience, and attention should also be paid to such quite fumbling attempts at inner spiritual experience, to a new interest in the spiritual world. But then the opposing spirits begin to stir.

After what has been printed about this, and after what such a representative of the spirit of the past has himself printed, he himself was recently supposed to have said some rather remarkable words here in Stuttgart about these attempts. On the one hand they are fumbling attempts to bring about a new religious interest and experience, and on the other are attempts to arrive at really new, concrete knowledge of the spiritual world in the way one tries to validate it through Anthroposophically oriented spiritual science.

I don't know how many of you saw the Shepherds Play† that was recently performed in the Waldorf School, where the one shepherd says he was almost dumbfounded because he had a spiritual vision.

Well, when I read the last page of Gogarten's "Spiritual Science and Christianity,"[†] I must say I was also almost dumbfounded; because one stands in amazement before the fact that it is possible that such things can be said at the present time. Just such things should stimulate one to consider a Cosmic New Year, to compare what is in the past with what is necessary in the future. For what did that man of religion actually say? I don't know if its heavy import was entirely understood. He said: "It is today—why am I saying today—it is always the most important task of piety to preserve those basic elements of which I spoke. Today we are almost completely lacking in that. We are stuck in religious 'interest' and in religious 'experience.' And since Anthroposophy is such good material for 'interest' and such a good medium for 'experience,' one is hard put to be able to resist it. One knows just so little any more of that ultimate basic tension that is brought into life by piety, which drives away every religious 'interest' and destroys every religious 'experience,' this tension between God and creature. And because one knows so little of this tension, therefore one knows just as little of the unconditional, direct oneness of God and man." Here we see every religious interest denigrated, every religious experience destroyed in the name of religion; and a quite vague tension, which of course cannot be further differentiated (which he does not want to differentiate any further) is supposed to take the place of religious interest and experience. One could become speechless when a representative of religion speaks in such a way, saying that true piety should drive away every religious interest, destroy every religious experience! So far have we come! And so far have we come that we do not perceive what lies behind it when an official representative of religion says:

Away with religious interest, away with religious experience!

You see, this man doesn't realize that he himself could never speak of religion if earlier there had not been atavistic religious interest and experience, that the gentleman could not stand in front of listeners as an official representative of religion if religion had not entered human development by way of religious interest and experience. And apart from all that, what I have just brought before you points to the fact that today, just those people who fancy themselves to be the true representatives of religious life are working for the destruction of religion's very existence. Have then these people lost any capacity to understand the human soul? Can these people no longer understand that everything that the human beings turn their attention to must be led by their interest, that everything that enters their consciousness must be carried by experience? It is even as if the human being no longer speaks out of such a consciousness, but only from the spirit of opposition. That is what in all seriousness should stand before our soul when we look into the mirror that so mysteriously uncovers the past and hides the future, yet still reveals it in a certain way that I have explained.

It is there that Anthroposophically oriented spiritual science wants to serve the religious interest, that it wants to bring content into religious experience. And what happens?

You see, during this year the question was put before the Holy Congregation of Cardinals whether the teachings today referred to as Anthroposophy can be reconciled with Catholic teachings, and whether it is permitted to join Theosophical societies, attend Theosophical meetings and to read Theosophical journals and newspapers. The answer was: No, to every point: "negative in omnibus." This is the spirit of opposition, and the Jesuit Zimmermann particularly interprets this decree of the Holy Congregation as applying to Anthroposophy. Now, what this Zimmermann writes[†] is probably familiar to you, and I don't need especially to explain it to you. But you must all surely know what wind, filled with the spirit of opposition, is blowing from a certain quarter today against Anthroposophically oriented spiritual science.

What kind of spirit is passing through the world in this wind? One can also feel it when one knows that the following words come from the pen of that same Zimmermann, who for years perpetuated the lie that I was formerly a priest who left the church: "With the defection of its General Secretary,[†] Dr. Rudolf Steiner, who took most of its members with him, the Theosophical Society, although initially very weakened, recovered itself somewhat over the years and now has about twenty-five lodges, about a fifth of which are dormant, and in Düsseldorf it publishes *Theosophical Striving* as its voice in Germany and Austria. The people around him complained that Steiner, who after his defection called his Theosophy 'Anthroposophy,' was becoming sterile, that he had no more visions, and was always lecturing about the same things, and would presumably soon latch onto something new," and so forth. And then there appears a subsequent article[†] in which the threefold idea is dealt with in an equally clever way. You see what kind of spirit of truth lies behind this Jesuit. What Jesuits say is not just their personal opinion, but the opinion of the Catholic Church, because each of them only speaks as one of its members. Therefore what he says relates back to the Catholic Church. Today these things must also be judged from a moral point of view. From a moral point of view one must ask whether someone who deals with the truth as he does, a man who in the present circumstances is indeed highly regarded within a particular religious community here on the Earth, could be so regarded by the true spirit of humanity. As long as questions of that kind cannot be addressed with the necessary seriousness, we have not yet arrived at a proper consideration of the Cosmic New Year. But it is necessary today that we arrive at a proper consideration of the Cosmic New Year. It is necessary that we extend the so-called compassion, which unfortunately often arises from egoistic sources, to the greater conditions of humanity and feel the compassion for humanity that will urge us on to make a spiritual movement like this one really fruitful for the development of humanity. Could you feel just on this day, my dear friends, that it is really the spirit of the world itself that for decades has wanted to enter in? Could you feel on this evening that here is a willingness to serve this spirit who wants to enter into humanity? Could you feel that this spirit is to be served here so that the souls of those who want to feel and to think together with this Anthroposophically oriented spiritual science feel united with the new spirit that wants to enter the world, this spirit that alone can bring an impulse of regeneration out of heaven to the self-destroying earthly world? In this hour—which in every year is symbolic, because in a way it calls upon us to experience it as the hour separating the past and the future—may you unite your souls with the new spirit, and experience in your souls that here the touching of the past year with the year to come is the touching of the world year that is ending its course with the world year that is about to spring forth!

But the passing world year will still send its aftereffects into the future; they will be destructive forces of a spiritual, legal, and economic kind. And it will be all the more necessary that as many people as possible will be taken up in the depths of their soul by the new year of a spiritual future, and will develop a will that can be the basis of building a new spiritual world into the future development of humanity. Those who want to kill off religious interest, who want to do away with religious experience will not care for the future of humanity. Only those who see how through our intellectual age the old religious interest has died away, the old religious life has been lamed, will see how a new religious experience must sprout up in humanity, so that human beings can bear the seeds of a future existence into the cosmos.

Lecture 5

STUTTGART, JANUARY 1, 1920

Today I would like to appear before you with New Year's greetings that contain what I would like to wish into your souls, what the present time needs so very much. May you recognize the great, urgent demands for the development of humankind, and may you cooperate, each in your own place and as much as you are able, in the fulfillment of what is so greatly needed by humanity in our time. At such a time that symbolically expresses the confluence of past and future, I may perhaps be allowed to refer to something that I believe, even though it is connected with personal experiences, has a certain significance for looking into the whole spiritual constitution of the present time.

My dear friends, in the near future essays of mine are to appear that I wrote a long time ago, some of them more than thirty years ago. Those essays that I wrote while still in Austria were collected through the love shown by our friend Dr. Kolisko† in undertaking this collection. Today in this consideration of the New Year (which may rightly also be a consideration of the times) I would like, as an introduction, to point out some of the things from those essays. What was written at that time was done in order to speak to the conscience, one can really say, of the German people, in order to give expression to what could then be perceived as a basic deficiency in the spiritual life of this German people. Allow me to read a few of these sentences, now more than thirty years old, from the article entitled "The Spiritual Signature of the Present."† (They point to a past of thirty years ago, which then was the present.) Standing within those symptoms of the general spiritual life that revealed itself mostly in the intellectual life of the nation, I wrote at that time: "With a shrug of the shoulder, our present generation† recalls that time when a philosophical impulse passed through all of German spiritual life. The mighty impulse of the time, which took hold of human spirits at the end of the last and the beginning of this century and which boldly set itself the highest thinkable tasks, now is ranked as a regrettable mistake. Whoever dares to take an opposing view when the talk is of 'Fichte's fantastic notions' or of Hegel's 'unreal playing with thoughts and words' is simply put down as a dilettante 'who has as little conception of the spirit of today's natural science as of the purity and strictness of the philosophical method.' At most Kant and Schopenhauer find favor with our contemporaries. The former succeeds in *apparently* deriving from his teachings the rather sparse philosophical crumbs that form the basis of modern science; the latter, besides his strictly scientific efforts, has also written works in an easy style and about things that are not beyond people with the most modest of spiritual horizons. But for that striving for the highest levels of the thought world, for that buoyancy of spirit that paralleled our classical cultural epoch, there is now lacking any sense or understanding. The seriousness of this phenomenon only becomes apparent when one considers that a lasting turning away from that spiritual direction would be for the Germans a loss of their self, a break with the folk spirit. For this striving arose from a deep need of the German character. It does not occur to us to want to deny the numerous mistakes made and biased opinions held by Fichte, Hegel, Schelling, Oken, and others in their bold undertakings in the realm of idealism; but we should not be mistaken about the sublime tendency that ensouled them, so right and fitting in a nation of thinkers. What characterizes the German is not the living sense for the immediate reality, for the external side of nature, which enabled the Greeks to produce their glorious imperishable creations—it is instead an incessant urgency of the spirit to find the reason for things, to find the apparently hidden, deeper causes of the nature that surrounds us. While the Greek spirit lived itself out in its wonderful world of forms and figures, the Germans—more withdrawn into themselves and having interaction less with nature, but therefore more with their heart and their own inner being—had to seek their conquests in the sphere of the world of pure thought. Therefore it was the *German* way in which Fichte and his successors confronted life and the world, and therefore their teachings had such an enthusiastic reception, and for a time the whole life of the nation was seized by it. But also therefore we must not break away from this direction of the spirit. Overcoming the mistakes, but a natural development on the basis that was established then, must be our watchword. Not what those spirits found, or thought they had found, but how they faced up to the problems of research—that is of lasting value."

At that time it should have been pointed out to the German people what was now threatening to disappear from their view. In those days one still lived in a different time than today: one lived in a time when it would have still been possible in certain circles, if one had wanted to, to connect oneself with the spirit that was beginning to decline and to act decisively to open a way for the development of new human impulses. However, human beings would have had to have been found then amongst those who called themselves leaders of the people, amongst those who were giving guidance to the youth for their later life. At that time there were no experiments of the kind that are now appearing in Russia; at that time those who were educators of the youth would have had the ability to turn back to the intentions of that former spiritual life and to let it arise again in a new form. But in those days no one wanted in the least to listen to a voice that spoke for such a revival of a truly spiritual striving of humanity. And everything that has characterized especially the lower and higher educators of the people in these last thirty years was an assault against the intentions of a spiritual view of the world. Today I must think about the fact that then, when I wrote those words, my interpretations of Goethe's worldview and his ideas about natural science[†] had just been published; and I must think how I then made those who are active in the field of thinking and of scientific research aware of two great dangers. I then formulated two terms to characterize the two great enemies of human spiritual progress. On the one hand I spoke of the dogma of revelation, and on the other hand I spoke of the dogma of mere experience. I wanted to show that the one-sided cultivation of the dogma of revelation as it has developed in confessional circles is just as harmful as the boasting about the so-called dogmas of experience, which means all of what is only provided by the outer sense world and the world of material facts by the natural scientists and sociologists. It was then my task, in the course of time, to formulate these ideas more concretely and to point out the real forces that lie behind these phenomena.

What lies behind what I called the dogma of revelation? All of what we today in a comprehensive way call the Luciferic influences on the course of human development. Whoever in our present time wants to lead humanity merely under the influence of the dogma of revelation is leading them in the sense of Lucifer; whoever (perhaps the natural scientists) wants to lead them merely in the sense of outer sensory experience, leads humanity in the sense of Ahriman. In our present serious time, may it not be a consideration for the New Year to cast an eye over the last three to four decades, to point out that it is just as essential for us today to raise once more the call that was raised then, only in a much stronger way?

My dear friends, by the course of external events these thirty to forty years have clearly shown how justified that call was at that time. Anyone who looks without prejudice at what has happened must say: if at that time such a call had become a reality in the minds of the people of Central Europe, what we now experience as misery and distress would not have come. At that time the call died away. Now one meets it coming from the Roman Holy Congregation in the decree of July 18, 1919,[†] and the cathedral chaplains announce that my writings on Anthroposophy may not be read because the Pope has forbidden it, so one must be instructed out of the writings of the opponents. The cathedral chaplains therefore refer not to my writings for knowledge about Anthroposophy, but to those of Seiling and his collaborators.[†] This is happening at the same time that, under the auspices of a Berlin government with socialist leanings,[†] negotiations are taking place for the establishment of a Roman Catholic nunciature in Berlin. This is also something that gives an indication of the spiritual signature of the present time.

And today one would really like to appeal already to the deepest heart forces of those who are still capable of feeling something of the spiritual impulses inherent in the development of humanity, so that they may wake up and really see how things are actually going. For today it is a question above all else of people finding the possibility of coming to their own self. And to come to one's self requires confidence in one's own strength of soul. It is just with this appeal to one's strength of soul that it is hard today to reach people. On the one hand people want to lean up against something that forces them from inside to think and want what is right, and on the other hand they want to lean against something that forces them from the outside to think and want what is right. People somehow always tend towards two such extremes and never want to exert themselves to strive for a balance between the forces emanating from these two extremes. Let us once more cast our eyes upon something of the spiritual signature of the present, which today is about to become a social and material signature. We hear arising in Eastern Europe the old Marxist cry: a new social order must come about among people where each human being can live according to his or her abilities and his or her needs.† A social order must be developed where the individual capacities of each human being become of value and where the justifiable needs of each human being can be satisfied. When thus abstractly announced, there is nothing in the least objectionable about this abstraction. But on the other hand we hear such a personality as Lenin† saying that such a social order cannot be established with the people of the present time—with them one can only set up a transitional social order. One can only establish something that of course will contain injustice in the widest sense. It is also present to an absurd degree in everything being established by Lenin and his followers: they believe one could only produce a new human race that does not yet exist by passing through this transitional phase, and when it comes to be, then one will be able to introduce into it that social order in which each person can make use of their capacities and live according to their needs. Thus, they invent a nonexistent human race in order to realize an idea that, as I said, is even justified in an abstract sense.

But could enough people not be found who grasp the whole seriousness of the current world situation when they hear something like
this? Is it not time for this sleepiness to cease, which closes its eyes
a little when something like this appears that in the deepest sense
points to the signature of the present, closes its eyes in order not to
fully take in the whole significance of such a thing in any way? To
come to a concrete understanding about these things, nothing else
helps than to abandon the ways of abstraction in the spiritual life.
But for that one must really first have a feeling for where abstraction
is present, when there is only talk in phrases about soul and spirit,
and one must be able to discern when soul and spirit are talked
about as a reality. You see, when one speaks of human capacities,
they appear as a manifestation of the inner being of the developing
person. Humanity is encouraged by a number of its representatives
to appropriately develop the capacities and forces that appear in the
maturing human being. We only perceive truly in this field if in a
certain way we perceive the manifestation of these forces and capacities as a manifestation of the divine. We must say to ourselves: the
human being has come out of a world of soul-spiritual being into
this world of sensory reality, and what expresses itself there as human
forces and capacities and what we have developed in ourselves and
in others originates in a spiritual world, and having descended
from a spiritual world into this physical human body, it has now
been incorporated in this body. But if you take the spirit and sense
of what has been explained here for decades, this spirit and sense
points out to you that with the incorporation of human capacities
and forces in the physical human body the possibility is given to the
Luciferic beings to access these capacities and forces.

We cannot do anything with these human capacities and forces
in the way of individual activity or activities in the sphere of education or culture without coming into touch with Luciferic forces. In
those regions that the human being passes through before entering
into physical existence through birth or conception, Luciferic powers
could not directly approach the human capacities and forces. The
incorporation in the human bodily system is the means whereby the
Luciferic powers can approach human capacities and forces. Only by

impartially facing up to this fact do we come to a right attitude in life to all that gushes forth in human nature as capacities and strengths. If we do not want to see the Luciferic, if we deny it, then we are trapped by it. But it is just then that we get into that state of mind that wants to deliver us entirely to something internally compelling, to be thus relieved by all kinds of mystical or religious powers from the necessity of appealing to the free self of the human being, and to seek the divine in the unfolding of our own free selves in the world.

People don't want to think for themselves—they want a vague power to express themselves from their inner being according to which they can prove themselves logical. They don't want to experience the truth, they don't want to exert themselves to have that inner, free experience that also experiences the truth. They want to experience the inner compulsion that compels them from within and expresses itself in the proof that does not appeal to experience, but to the power of something spiritual that will overpower and force them to think this or that about nature and about the human being. But in appealing to this inner compulsion, this inner power, people are delivering themselves up to the Luciferic powers. The means that can be used so that people appeal to this compulsion, so that they do not raise themselves to stand freely within the spiritual world, are to forbid them to think that the human being consists of body, soul, and spirit, as was done by the Eighth General Council of Constantinople,[†] and to do away with any concern for the spirit. These are coincidences that must no longer be overlooked today, and must be clearly and impartially looked at. At that time, in the year 869, when it was decided that people must no longer believe in the spirit of the human being, the inclination toward Lucifer entered European civilization. And today we have the fulfillment of that. People have given in long enough to the inclination not to experience the truth, but to allow the compulsion of proof, of impersonal proof to act upon them.

That has thrown them to the other extreme. People have not learned to occupy themselves in a pertinent way with the human capacities and forces and have not wanted to admit that Luciferic powers live in the human capacities and forces when they are incorporated in the physical body in the way I have just explained. Thereby people have experienced the wrong attitude towards the individual capacities and forces to which modern humanity has come, which is currently the order of the day.

At the other pole of the human being are human needs, those needs that initially express themselves in the purely physical nature. In his *Aesthetic Letters* Schiller† contrasted these needs so beautifully with the abstract logical power and called them the essential need ("Notdurft"), while he characterized the logical compulsion as the other power, the power deviating into the spiritual. At that time, during the great period of German development, such a personality as Schiller was on the way to correctly understand the contrasting polarity of the human being. Then the time was not yet ripe to say more than was said by Schiller, Goethe, and those of like mind. Our new time is faced with the necessity to build these things further, and then it becomes Anthroposophically oriented spiritual science. Those who only know the one-sided power of proof in the spiritual sphere, in their lives also only learn to know the one-sided driving force of nature in human needs. You can easily imagine, when human beings enter into the physical-sensory world with their capacities and forces through conception or birth, and Lucifer comes over them and takes something that the human beings themselves should have, on the one side, on the side of the head, so to speak, then there also remains for the human beings themselves a lesser capacity to assert their independence in the sphere of their needs. Through what Lucifer appropriates for himself on the one hand, Ahriman on the other hand gains the possibility of appropriating what is at work in the needs of human nature. And so along with that possibility and the dogma of mere outer sensory experience, the door is opened to the penetration by Ahriman of the instinctive life of humanity in the last third of the nineteenth century. And so, in not realizing that healing lies in the equilibrium between the two extremes, between the capacities on the one hand and the needs on the other, modern humanity stands before a dreadful fact. Out of its materialistic mind it only looks upon the body that produces the capacities, meaning only upon the Luciferic origin of the capacities—because through the fact that the capacities enter into the body, they become Luciferic, and when one believes that the capacities come from the body, then one believes in Lucifer. And when one believes the needs arise from the body, then one only believes in what is Ahrimanic in those needs.

And what experiment is currently being made over in Eastern Europe under the guidance of the West? This guidance not only appears so obvious because Lenin and Trotsky[†] are spiritual students of the West, but also because Lenin was dispatched to Russia in a leaded coach with Dr. Helphand,[†] so that what is called Bolshevism was imported goods from the German government and the German High Command. What is being attempted there in the Eastern European culture? There it is attempted to eliminate everything that is human, everything that incorporates itself as human in the human body—to harness Lucifer and Ahriman together in their cultural purity. If this were realized today in the East, then a creation would result from the joint efforts of Ahriman and Lucifer with the exclusion of everything appropriate to the human being. People would be harnessed into the Luciferic-Ahrimanic culture like a part of a machine in the whole mechanism of this machine—only a machine part is lifeless and lets itself be harnessed, while human nature is inwardly alive, ensouled, and inspirited and does not fit into a merely Luciferic-Ahrimanic organization, and therefore must perish.

Only through spiritual science can we understand what is actually happening today in this spiritually most nebulous of materialistic worlds. But only with this spiritual-scientific perception and the seriousness living within it can be understood what it means that in the last thirty to forty years we have not wanted to turn back within the German character to the German spirituality which is referred to here in my essay. On the contrary, we have finally come so far in this German cultural world that authority has become vested in those who considered it right to let the inaugurators of Lucifer and Ahriman be sent to Russia in a leaded coach, and indeed by a man who was in their service, and who became, through all the services he rendered by thus mediating between East and West, a man who during this time built himself a villa in Constantinople, another in Switzerland, and a third in Copenhagen. It doesn't do today, just to casually look around, in order to be able to sleep well, in view of what is actually happening in the depths of today's world. It should be felt today how necessary it is to say: we have denied and stomped underfoot what was created in the German spiritual life at the time of Schiller and Goethe, and we have the task to start there and to continue to build. We cannot pour any better New Year's thoughts into our souls than the intention to reconnect with that.

In that place (and I have already mentioned this many years ago) where now our friend Dr. Kolisko has collected my essays, there lived in the 1860s and 1870s a man called Heinrich Deinhardt,[†] who was a Viennese pedagogue. In an age that was descending into materialism, he had the spirit to take hold of pedagogy from the standpoint of Schiller's *Aesthetic Letters*. He wrote beautiful explanatory letters about Schiller's *Aesthetic Letters*, describing how human beings should be taught to free themselves from compulsory logical necessity and the necessities only arising from instincts; these letters were published at that time. He was one of those who warned humanity, saying: what otherwise must take place must be prevented by means of education. He had not yet been able to speak using spiritual-scientific concepts, but with his words he pointed out at that time how the Luciferic-Ahrimanic culture would arise if humanity did not shape the science and the art of education according to a condition of balance. This man, Heinrich Deinhardt, had the misfortune at that time in Vienna to be knocked down in the street and break his leg, something that could have been healed with a simple operation. However, according to his doctors he was so poorly nourished that the process of healing could not be completed. And so this man, who already saw quite deeply into what was going on in his time, died as a result of a small accident. Yes, that was the way people in Central Europe were treated who wanted to find something out of spirituality. This example could be multiplied many times.

Now, those who write like the Jesuit father Zimmermann I mentioned yesterday will probably not die of hunger: "Also, for example, it is boasted[†] in the weekly *Threefold Social Organism*, No. 6,[†] that the 'new impulse' (a favorite expression of the Anthroposophists and the 'Threefolders') is based on the 'fullness of Steiner's spiritual knowledge.' The manager of the Waldorf-Astoria cigarette factory in Stuttgart has founded the 'Free Waldorf School'† for the children of the employees and workers of the enterprise, 'inspired by all that has come to him from the thoughts of Dr. Steiner's Anthroposophically oriented spiritual science.' There, 'Anthroposophy is to be the artistic educational method.'" Those who mock and want to tread into the dust what wants to come forth from the spirit of the time will also not die of hunger in our present hard times. But it will be very necessary indeed that we imprint such New Year's impulses into the soul that will ensure that we do not sleepily and carelessly pass by what is really happening. Above all, we must energetically take up what is strongly emphasized by Anthroposophically oriented spiritual science. Oh, I see quite a few in our own ranks who would most love to sleep through those things that reveal themselves out of great compassion, out of pity for what in our time, if it were left to itself, must lead to ruin! There are weak souls who enroll in this Anthroposophical Society and who say: yes, spiritual science, that I like; but I don't want to know anything about social activity, that doesn't belong in there. They could take an example from the opponents. The Jesuit father Zimmermann follows everything that we do! He ends his article by saying: "The weekly *Threefold Organism*, No. 8, certainly means that here there was an 'attempt by the Church to destroy' the historical task of the self-determination of the individual." And also in other articles the Jesuit father Zimmermann has shown that he concerns himself with everything that goes on with us.

So one would wish that those in our own ranks would also concern themselves about things in a positive sense. You see, I would like to say that the watchers, who only see how they can discover any kind of weakness in the field of Anthroposophically oriented spiritual science and what arises from it, are not few in number—but I think you know I am not so foolish as to refer to something of the sort I am about to mention out of vanity, and therefore I can also dare to do so. Of course the opponents' side would like to easily find a point of attack here and there. It is surely good then to be able to read in the essay that Dr. Rittelmeyer† wrote on "Steiner, War, and Revolution":† "Just in these days I spoke with a young Swedish scholar of political economy from the school of the strict national economist Cassel,† who said to me he had read Steiner's book from cover to cover in the expectation of being able to unmask him as a dilettante; but he had not succeeded in finding him guilty of any errors." Yes, more consideration should be given to such things in our circles. We should build on the basis of the knowledge that what is intended here has nothing to do with the customary idle talk of Theosophy that takes place here and there, but which is based on just as strict a judgment about things as any science that has ever established its worth. If something like that were thoroughly appreciated, then one would also know why what happened is now called a defection by Father Zimmermann. You know that that was not the case, but that we were thrown out because we did not succeed in bringing a real seriousness into this society of wishy-washy talk—because there a real seriousness was not wanted, because there they wanted to continue to chatter on in the same way as they had chattered for years, at best in connection with something or other about which one can say all kinds of things without having any knowledge of the spiritual world. What our time so urgently needs is complete seriousness in the area of spiritual life. Since my being here in these days is coming to an end, I wanted to speak again about this complete seriousness on this New Year's Day, and I would very much wish that a New Year's resolution that each person can only make for themselves will be there among us: namely, that through the hearts and minds of our friends eyes are opened for the vision of what is desperately needed, opened for what can only come from the spirit alone in order to help humanity. Today we cannot bring about healing with the existing outer arrangements; we must impress something new into the development of humanity. This must be recognized. And to feel that it must be recognized is surely the worthiest New Year's thought that can arise in your hearts today, at the beginning of the year 1920, which will bring many important decisions if people are found who recognize what humanity needs, as it was indicated today. It must be recognized that the year 1920 will bring want and misery if such people are not found, and only those have the say who want to continue working on in the same old way.

EDITORIAL AND REFERENCE NOTES

Note on the text: At the end of December 1919 Rudolf Steiner gave numerous lectures in Stuttgart: *The Light Course* (CW 320); *The Genius of Language* (CW 299); also the five lectures to members in this volume. Furthermore there were conferences with the Teachers' Collegium of the Free Waldorf School. Everything was taken down stenographically and translated into normal text. However it is not known who had taken notes on a particular occasion and whose notes were then printed. It also happened that the note takers later sat down together and jointly worked out a text. It is known that of those who were stenographers, Clara Michels, Hedda Hummel, and Frank Seiler were then in Stuttgart. The original stenographic notes were not preserved. The printed text is therefore based on the typewritten version produced at that time.

Page 1, "The last lectures held here"
Seventeen lectures are meant, given in Stuttgart from April 21 to September 28, 1919, partly printed in *Geisteswissenschaftliche Behandlung sozialer und pädagogischer Fragen* (GA 192).

Page 4, "the threefolding of the social realm"
Compare *Towards Social Renewal* (CW 23) and *World Economy* (CW 340).

Page 6, "Tagore"
Rabindranath Tagore (1861-1941), Bengali poet, Brahmo Samaj (Hindu reformist) philosopher, visual artist, playwright, novelist, composer, teacher, and widely respected sage, whose works in translation were published in many languages, especially after he won the Nobel prize for Literature in 1913.

Page 10, "barren state of contemporary spiritual life"
Compare the reports of the lecture in Basel on September 25, 1912, printed in *The History and Contents of the First Section of the Esoteric School 1904-1914* (CW 264), where it says: "Ram Mohan Roy was the founder of the Bramo Samaj [Hindu Reform Movement]…[which] had Arya Samaj as an offshoot. H.P. Blavatsky and Olcott moved to India in 1878 to join this association and expecting much good to come from it.…"

Page 12, "Newton, Darwin, Mill, Spencer, and Hume"
Sir Isaac Newton (1643-1727), English physicist, mathematician, and astronomer.
Charles Robert Darwin (1809-1882), English natural scientist, author of the theory of evolution named after him.
John Stuart Mill (1806-1873), English philosopher and politician.
Herbert Spencer (1820-1903), English philosopher.
David Hume (1711-1776), Scottish philosopher and historian.

Page 13, "Wilhelm von Humboldt"
(1767-1835), diplomat, linguist, and, for a time, Prussian Minister of
Education, wrote *On the Limits of State Action* in 1792 (first published in 1851
in German).

Page 14, "Russian revolutionaries"
So far not identified.

Page 15, "Dr. Stein"
Walter Johannes Stein (1891-1957), teacher at the Waldorf School in Stuttgart,
author and lecturer.

Page 16, "The periodical"
Dreigliederung des sozialen Organismus [The threefold social organism], published
by the Bund für Dreigliederung des sozialen Organismus [Association for the
Threefold Social Organism], Stuttgart 1919-1923. The statement referred to
appears in year 1, No. 21, Stuttgart, 1919.

Page 16, "Seiling"
Max Seiling (1852-1928) was at first a follower of Rudolf Steiner, then an
opponent.

Page 16, "Dr. Boos"
Roman Boos (1889-1952), national economist and author.

Page 16, "What a way it is from the clear thoughts of Waxweiler"
The reference is to Emile Waxweiler, Director of the Institut de Sociologie in
Brussels, author of *Esquisse d'une sociologie*, Bruxelles and Paris, 1906, and *La
Belgique neutre et loyale*. The article is by Adolphe Ferrière, another sociologist
of the time: "La loi du progres economique et la justice sociale" in the periodical
Suisse-Belgique Outremer Year 1. No. 3-4, July-August, 1919, p. 19.

Page 16, "Wilhelm II"
Wilhelm II (1859-1941), German Emperor from 1888 to 1918.

Page 17, "Rasputin"
Grigorie Jefimowitsch Rasputin, the Russian monk who exerted influence at the
Russian court, particularly with the Tsarina.

Page 19, "David Friedrich Strauss"
David Friedrich Strauss (1808-1874), German theologian and writer who scan-
dalized Europe with his portrayal of the "historical Jesus," whose divine nature
he denied. His two main works are *The Life of Jesus* and *The Christian Doctrine
of Faith, Its Doctrinal Development and Conflict with Modern Science*. Also *The
Old and the New Faith*, 1872, in German.

Page 20 "Tirpitz book"
Alfred von Tirpitz (1849-1930), Grand Admiral, Commander of the German Navy during World War I. *Erinerungen* [Memoirs], 1920.

Page 20, "Ludendorff book"
Erich Ludendorff (1865-1937), Hindenburg's Chief of the General Staff in World War I, First Quartermaster-General, 1916; discharged in 1918 for his determination to continue the war. Took part in the "Hitlerputsch" on November 8, 1923. Author of *Meine Kriegs-erinnerungen 1914-1918* [My war memoirs, 1914-1918], 1919.

Page 21, "Adolf Harnack"
Adolf von Harnack (1851-1930), German Protestant church historian. *Das Wesen des Christentums* [The nature of Christianity], 16 lectures at the University of Berlin, 1899-1900.

Page 21, "I have often spoken to you here"
For example, in the lecture of September 8, 1919, in *Geisteswissenschaftliche Behandlung sozialer und pädagogischer Fragen* (GA 192).

Page 25, "Wilson ... Fourteen Points"
President Wilson's message to the US Congress of January 8, 1919, with fourteen points, which were to regulate the coexistence of the nations after the war, made a strong impression on the people of the world. The last point concerned the formation of a universal league of nations.

Page 26, "I am with you always, even until the end of the world."
Matthew 28:20.

Page 27, "Milton's *Paradise Lost*"
John Milton (1608-1674), *Paradise Lost*, 1667.

Page 27, "Klopstock's *Messiah*"
Friedrich Gottfried Klopstock (1724-1803), German poet. *Messiah*, 20 cantos, 1748-73.

Page 28, "in my booklet *Goethe's Spiritual Nature*"
The actual title is *Goethe's Spiritual Nature and its Revelation in "Faust" and through "The Fairy Tale of The Snake and the Lily,"* 1918 (CW 22).

Page 28, "Leonardo da Vinci"
Leonardo da Vinci (1452-1519), Italian painter, scholar, and engineer.

Page 31, "We have often characterized it"
Compare, for example, "Erdensterben und Weltenleben" [Earthly death and cosmic life], third lecture in GA 192.

Page 32, "If in our brain only upbuilding processes were at work"
See "Erdensterben und Weltenleben" [Earthly death and cosmic life], the third
lecture in GA 192.

Page 37, "Nietzsche ... an opponent of Socrates"
See Friedrich Nietzsche, *Philosophy in the Tragic Age of the Greeks* (1873).

Page 39, "to what I call Schmiedelei"
Otto Schmiedel (1858-?), Protestant theologian, see his book *The Principle
Problems of the Study of the Life of Jesus*, Tubingen, 1902.

Page 39, "our Dr. Schmiedel"
Dr. Oskar Schmiedel (1887-1959), chemist.

Page 41, "Traub"
Friedrich Traub, Professor in Tubingen. *Rudolf Steiner als Philosoph und Theosoph*
[Rudolf Steiner as philosopher and Theosophist], Tubingen, 1919.

Page 47, "Shepherds Play"
This refers to the so-called *Oberüfer Shepherds Play*, collected by Steiner's mentor
Karl Julius Schroer from the Palatinate (Rhineland) and still performed in
Waldorf Schools.

Page 48, "the last page of Gogarten's 'Spiritual Science and Christianity'"
Friedrich Gogarten (1887-1931), German Protestant theologian, a principal
representative of dialectical theology. Wrote *Rudolf Steiners 'Geisteswissenschaft'
und das Christentum* [Rudolf Steiner's spiritual science and Christianity].
Investigations concerning questions of faith and life among the educated of all
classes, Brochure No. 2, published by the Evangelische Volksbund, Stuttgart,
1920.

Page 49, "what this Zimmermann writes"
Otto Zimmermann, S.J., polemicized for years against Rudolf Steiner and
Anthroposophy in the Catholic periodicals *Stimmen aus Maria Laach* [Voices
from Maria Laach] and *Stimmen der Zeit* [Voices of the time].

Page 49, "With the defection of its General Secretary"
"Die kirchliche Verurteilung der Theosophie" [The church's condemnation of
Theosophy] in *Stimmen der Zeit* [Voices of the time], Freiburg im Breisgau, Vol.
98, 50th year, No. 2, November 1919, p. 149.

Page 50, "And then there appears a subsequent article"
Allusion to the article "Dreigliederung des sozialen Organismus?" [The threefold
social organism] by Constantin Noppel, S.J., in the previously mentioned issue
of *Stimmen der Zeit*.

Page 52, "Dr. Kolisko"
Eugen Kolisko (1893-1939), physician and teacher at the Waldorf School in Stuttgart.

Page 52, "The 'Spiritual Signature of the Present'"
(Here Steiner is referring to his article on the loss of German Idealism: In *Deutsche Wochenschrift* [German weekly], Berlin, Vienna, 1888, No. 24, which was republished in the periodical *Dreigliederung des sozialen Organismus* [Threefold social organism], vol. 3, number 37, Stuttgart, 1922. Reprinted in *Methodische Grundlagen der Anthroposophie 1889-1901* (GA 30).

Page 53, "With a shrug of the shoulder, our present generation"
See previous reference to *Deutsche Wochenschrift* [German weekly].

Page 54, "my interpretations of Goethe's worldview and his ideas about natural science"
See *Nature's Open Secret* (CW 1). Also *A Theory of Knowledge Based on Goethe's World Conception* (CW 2); *Goethe's Worldview* (CW 6); and *Goethe's Spiritual Nature and its Revelation in "Faust" and through "The Fairy Tale of the Snake and the Lily"'* (CW 22).

Page 55, "decree of July 18, 1919"
The question before the Congregation of The Holy Office on July 18, 1919, was as follows: "Whether the teachings, which today are called Theosophical, can be reconciled with Catholic teachings and if it is therefore permitted to join Theosophical societies, attend their meetings, read their books, newspapers, periodicals, and writings...?" The answer was: "No, in every case"—*Negative in Omnibus* (Acta Apostolica Sedis ll, 1919, 317). Compare: "Die kirchliche Verurteilung der Theosophie" [The church's condemnation of Theosophy], in *Stimmen der Zeit* [Voices of the time], Freiburg im Breisgau, vol. 98, 50th year, issue No. 2, Nov. 1919, p. 150. Otto Zimmermann and other Catholic clergy then extended this decision to also include Anthroposophical writings.

Page 55, "Seiling and his collaborators"
Max Seiling (1852-1928) was at first a follower of Rudolf Steiner, then an opponent.

Page 55, "a Berlin government with socialist leanings"
During the time of the Armistice and the peace negotiations the German government consisted basically of an uncertain coalition of the Social Democratic Party and the so-called Catholic Center. This delicate balance was influenced by numerous groups and personalities from the most diverse camps. See Gerhard Schultz, *Revolutionen und Friedensschlüsse 1917-1920* [Revolutions and peace agreements]. Deutscher Taschenbuch Verlag series on world history in the twentieth century, Vol. 2, 1967.

Page 56, "each human being can live according to his or her abilities and his or her needs"
Lenin cited in "Staat und Revolution" [State and revolution], p. 145, from the *Kritik des Gothaer Programms* [Critique of the Gothaer program] by Karl Marx, in which it says: "… after the general development of individuals, the means of production have also grown, and the wellsprings of societal wealth give greater flow—only then can the narrow horizon of civil rights be crossed over, and society can write on its banners: Each according to his abilities and to each according to his needs!"

Page 56, "Lenin"
Vladimir Ilyich Ulyanov (1870-1924), known as Lenin, founder and leader of Bolshevism.

Page 58, "the Eighth General Council of Constantinople"
At this council, in the year 869, it was established in the "Canones contra Photium" under Canon 11 that the human being does not have "two souls," but "one soul rational and intellectual."

Page 59, "In his *Aesthetic Letters*, Schiller"
Friedrich Schiller (1759-1805), *On the Aesthetic Education of Man* (1793-95).

Page 60, "Trotsky"
Leon Davidovich Bronstein (1879-1940), known as Trotsky. Russian Bolshevist leader, supplanted by Stalin, later driven into exile and assassinated in Mexico by the Russian Secret Service.

Page 60, "Dr. Helphand"
Alexander Helphand called himself Parvus Helphand. Russian socialist, and, for a time, a political refugee in Germany. Chief editor of the *Sachsische Arbeiterzeitung* [Saxon workers newspaper], Dresden. In the First World War he played a significant role in bringing about the Russian Revolution, as well as the peace Treaty of Brest-Litovsk (1918). See Georg Wolf, *Warten aufs letzte Gefecht* [Waiting for the last battle], Cologne, 1961.

Page 61, "Heinrich Deinhardt"
Beiträge zur Würdigung Schillers, Briefe über die ästhetische Erziehung des Menschen [Contributions toward an appreciation of Schiller's 'On the Aesthetic Education of Man'], Stuttgart, 1922.

Page 61, "Also, for example, it is boasted"
"Die kirchliche Verurteilung der Theosophie" [The church's condemnation of Theosophy], in *Stimmen der Zeit*, Freiburg im Breisgau, Vol. 98, 50th year, Issue No. 2, Nov. 1919, p. 149.

Page 61, "In the weekly *Threefold Social Organism*"
See the note for page 16.

Page 62, "the Free Waldorf School"
The Free Waldorf School in Stuttgart was founded in the year 1919 by Emil Molt, under the pedagogical leadership of Rudolf Steiner who also appointed the faculty and gave them seminar courses to prepare them.

Page 62, "Dr. Rittelmeyer"
Friedrich Rittelmeyer (1872-1938), Protestant theologian, co-founder of The Christian Community and its leader until his death.

Page 62, "'Steiner, War, and Revolution'"
Reprint from *Christentum und Gegenwart* [Christianity and today], a periodical, Nurnberg, 1919.

Page 63, "Cassel"
Gustav Cassel (1886-1945), Swedish national economist.

RUDOLF STEINER'S COLLECTED WORKS

The German Edition of Rudolf Steiner's Collected Works (the Gesamtausgabe [GA] published by Rudolf Steiner Verlag, Dornach, Switzerland) presently runs to over 354 titles, organized either by type of work (written or spoken), chronology, audience (public or other), or subject (education, art, etc.). For ease of comparison, the Collected Works in English [CW] follows the German organization exactly. A complete listing of the CWs follows with literal translations of the German titles. Other than in the case of the books published in his lifetime, titles were rarely given by Rudolf Steiner himself, and were often provided by the editors of the German editions. The titles in English are not necessarily the same as the German; and, indeed, over the past seventy-five years have frequently been different, with the same book sometimes appearing under different titles.

For ease of identification and to avoid confusion, we suggest that readers looking for a title should do so by CW number. Because the work of creating the Collected Works of Rudolf Steiner is an ongoing process, with new titles being published every year, we have not indicated in this listing which books are presently available. To find out what titles in the Collected Works are currently in print, please check our website at www.steinerbooks.org, or write to SteinerBooks 610 Main Street, Great Barrington, MA 01230:

Written Work

CW 13   Occult Science in Outline

CW 14   Four Mystery Dramas

CW 15   The Spiritual Guidance of the Individual and Humanity

CW 16   A Way to Human Self-Knowledge: Eight Meditations

CW 17   The Threshold of the Spiritual World. Aphoristic Comments

CW 18   The Riddles of Philosophy in Their History, Presented as an Outline

CW 19   Contained in CW 24

CW 20   The Riddles of the Human Being: Articulated and Unarticulated in the Thinking, Views and Opinions of a Series of German and Austrian Personalities

CW 21   The Riddles of the Soul

CW 22   Goethe's Spiritual Nature And Its Revelation In "Faust" and through the "Fairy Tale of the Snake and the Lily"

CW 23   The Central Points of the Social Question in the Necessities of Life in the Present and the Future

CW 24   Essays Concerning the Threefold Division of the Social Organism and the Period 1915-1921

CW 25   Cosmology, Religion and Philosophy

CW 26   Anthroposophical Leading Thoughts

CW 27   Fundamentals for Expansion of the Art of Healing according to Spiritual-Scientific Insights

CW 28   The Course of My Life

CW 29   Collected Essays on Dramaturgy, 1889-1900

CW 30   Methodical Foundations of Anthroposophy: Collected Essays on Philosophy, Natural Science, Aesthetics and Psychology, 1884-1901

CW 31   Collected Essays on Culture and Current Events, 1887-1901

CW 32   Collected Essays on Literature, 1884-1902

CW 33   Biographies and Biographical Sketches, 1894-1905

CW 34   Lucifer-Gnosis: Foundational Essays on Anthroposophy and Reports from the Periodicals "Lucifer" and "Lucifer-Gnosis," 1903-1908

CW 35   Philosophy and Anthroposophy: Collected Essays, 1904-1923

CW 36   The Goetheanum-Idea in the Middle of the Cultural Crisis of the Present: Collected Essays from the Periodical "Das Goetheanum," 1921-1925

CW 37   Now in CWs 260a and 251

CW 38   Letters, Vol. 1: 1881-1890

CW 39   Letters, Vol. 2: 1890-1925

CW 40   Truth-Wrought Words

CW 40a   Sayings, Poems and Mantras; Supplementary Volume

CW 42   Now in CWs 264-266

Lectures to the Members of the Anthroposophical Society

CW 224   The Human Soul and its Connection with Divine-Spiritual Individualities. The Internalization of the Festivals of the Year

CW 225   Three Perspectives of Anthroposophy. Cultural Phenomena observed from a Spiritual-Scientific Perspective

CW 226   Human Being, Human Destiny, and World Development

CW 227   Initiation-Knowledge

CW 228   Science of Initiation and Knowledge of the Stars. The Human Being in the Past, the Present, and the Future from the Viewpoint of the Development of Consciousness

CW 229   The Experiencing of the Course of the Year in Four Cosmic Imaginations

CW 230   The Human Being as Harmony of the Creative, Building, and Formative World-Word

CW 231   The Supersensible Human Being, Understood Anthroposophically

CW 232   The Forming of the Mysteries

CW 233   World History Illuminated by Anthroposophy and as the Foundation for Knowledge of the Human Spirit

CW 233a   Mystery Sites of the Middle Ages: Rosicrucianism and the Modern Initiation-Principle. The Festival of Easter as Part of the History of the Mysteries of Humanity

CW 234   Anthroposophy. A Summary after 21 Years

CW 235   Esoteric Observations of Karmic Relationships in 6 Volumes, Vol. 1

CW 236   Esoteric Observations of Karmic Relationships in 6 Volumes, Vol. 2

CW 237   Esoteric Observations of Karmic Relationships in 6 Volumes, Vol. 3: The Karmic Relationships of the Anthroposophical Movement

CW 238   Esoteric Observations of Karmic Relationships in 6 Volumes, Vol. 4: The Spiritual Life of the Present in Relationship to the Anthroposophical Movement

CW 239   Esoteric Observations of Karmic Relationships in 6 Volumes, Vol. 5

CW 240   Esoteric Observations of Karmic Relationships in 6 Volumes, Vol. 6

CW 243   The Consciousness of the Initiate

CW 245   Instructions for an Esoteric Schooling

CW 250   The Building-Up of the Anthroposophical Society. From the Beginning to the Outbreak of the First World War

CW 251   The History of the Goetheanum Building-Association

CW 252   Life in the Anthroposophical Society from the First World War to the Burning of the First Goetheanum

CW 253   The Problems of Living Together in the Anthroposophical Society. On the Dornach Crisis of 1915. With Highlights on Swedenborg's Clairvoyance, the Views of Freudian Psychoanalysts, and the Concept of Love in Relation to Mysticism

CW 319   Anthroposophical Knowledge of the Human Being and Medicine
CW 320   Spiritual-Scientific Impulses for the Development of Physics 1:
          The First Natural-Scientific Course: Light, Color, Tone, Mass,
          Electricity, Magnetism
CW 321   Spiritual-Scientific Impulses for the Development of Physics 2:
          The Second Natural-Scientific Course: Warmth at the Border of
          Positive and Negative Materiality
CW 322   The Borders of the Knowledge of Nature
CW 323   The Relationship of the various Natural-Scientific Fields to
          Astronomy
CW 324   Nature Observation, Mathematics, and Scientific
          Experimentation and Results from the Viewpoint of
          Anthroposophy
CW 324a   The Fourth Dimension in Mathematics and Reality
CW 325   Natural Science and the World-Historical Development of
          Humanity since Ancient Times
CW 326   The Moment of the Coming Into Being of Natural Science in
          World History and Its Development Since Then
CW 327   Spiritual-Scientific Foundations for Success in Farming. The
          Agricultural Course
CW 328   The Social Question
CW 329   The Liberation of the Human Being as the Foundation for a
          New Social Form
CW 330   The Renewal of the Social Organism
CW 331   Work-Council and Socialization
CW 332   The Alliance for Threefolding and the Total Reform of Society.
          The Council on Culture and the Liberation of the Spiritual Life
CW 332a   The Social Future
CW 333   Freedom of Thought and Social Forces
CW 334   From the Unified State to the Threefold Social Organism
CW 335   The Crisis of the Present and the Path to Healthy Thinking
CW 336   The Great Questions of the Times and Anthroposophical
          Spiritual Knowledge
CW 337a   Social Ideas, Social Reality, Social Practice, Vol. 1: Question-
          and- Answer Evenings and Study Evenings of the Alliance for the
          Threefold Social Organism in Stuttgart, 1919-1920
CW 337b   Social Ideas, Social Realities, Social Practice, Vol. 2: Discussion
          Evenings of the Swiss Alliance for the Threefold Social Organism
CW 338   How Does One Work on Behalf of the Impulse for the Threefold
          Social Organism?
CW 339   Anthroposophy, Threefold Social Organism, and the Art of
          Public Speaking
CW 340   The National-Economics Course. The Tasks of a New Science of
          Economics, Volume 1

SIGNIFICANT EVENTS
IN THE LIFE OF RUDOLF STEINER

1829: June 23: birth of Johann Steiner (1829-1910)—Rudolf Steiner's father—in Geras, Lower Austria.

1834: May 8: birth of Franciska Blie (1834-1918)—Rudolf Steiner's mother—in Horn, Lower Austria. "My father and mother were both children of the glorious Lower Austrian forest district north of the Danube."

1860: May 16: marriage of Johann Steiner and Franciska Blie.

1861: February 25: birth of *Rudolf Joseph Lorenz Steiner* in Kraljevec, Croatia, near the border with Hungary, where Johann Steiner works as a telegrapher for the South Austria Railroad. Rudolf Steiner is baptized two days later, February 27, the date usually given as his birthday.

1862: Summer: the family moves to Mödling, Lower Austria.

1863: The family moves to Pottschach, Lower Austria, near the Styrian border, where Johann Steiner becomes stationmaster. "The view stretched to the mountains...majestic peaks in the distance and the sweet charm of nature in the immediate surroundings."

1864: November 15: birth of Rudolf Steiner's sister, Leopoldine (d. November 1, 1927). She will become a seamstress and live with her parents for the rest of her life.

1866: July 28: birth of Rudolf Steiner's deaf-mute brother, Gustav (d. May 1, 1941).

1867: Rudolf Steiner enters the village school. Following a disagreement between his father and the schoolmaster, whose wife falsely accused the boy of causing a commotion, Rudolf Steiner is taken out of school and taught at home.

1868: A critical experience. Unknown to the family, an aunt dies in a distant town. Sitting in the station waiting room, Rudolf Steiner sees her "form," which speaks to him, asking for help. "Beginning with this experience, a new soul life began in the boy, one in which not only the outer trees and mountains spoke to him, but also the worlds that lay behind them. From this moment on, the boy began to live with the spirits of nature...."

1869: The family moves to the peaceful, rural village of Neudorfl, near Wiener-Neustadt in present-day Hungary. Rudolf Steiner attends the village school. Because of the "unorthodoxy" of his writing and spelling, he has to do "extra lessons."

1870: Through a book lent to him by his tutor, he discovers geometry: "To grasp something purely in the spirit brought me inner happiness. I know that I first learned happiness through geometry." The same tutor allows him to draw, while other students still struggle with their reading and writing. "An artistic element" thus enters his education.

1871:   Though his parents are not religious, Rudolf Steiner becomes a "church child," a favorite of the priest, who was "an exceptional character." "Up to the age of ten or eleven, among those I came to know, he was far and away the most significant." Among other things, he introduces Steiner to Copernican, heliocentric cosmology. As an altar boy, Rudolf Steiner serves at Masses, funerals, and Corpus Christi processions. At year's end, after an incident in which he escapes a thrashing, his father forbids him to go to church.

1872:   Rudolf Steiner transfers to grammar school in Wiener-Neustadt, a five-mile walk from home, which must be done in all weathers.

1873-75: Through his teachers and on his own, Rudolf Steiner has many wonderful experiences with science and mathematics. Outside school, he teaches himself analytic geometry, trigonometry, differential equations, and calculus.

1876:   Rudolf Steiner begins tutoring other students. He learns bookbinding from his father. He also teaches himself stenography.

1877:   Rudolf Steiner discovers Kant's *Critique of Pure Reason*, which he reads and rereads. He also discovers and reads von Rotteck's *World History*.

1878:   He studies extensively in contemporary psychology and philosophy.

1879:   Rudolf Steiner graduates from high school with honors. His father is transferred to Inzersdorf, near Vienna. He uses his first visit to Vienna "to purchase a great number of philosophy books"— Kant, Fichte, Schelling, and Hegel, as well as numerous histories of philosophy. His aim: to find a path from the "I" to nature.

October 1879-1883: Rudolf Steiner attends the Technical College in Vienna—to study mathematics, chemistry, physics, mineralogy, botany, zoology, biology, geology, and mechanics—with a scholarship. He also attends lectures in history and literature, while avidly reading philosophy on his own. His two favorite professors are Karl Julius Schröer (German language and literature) and Edmund Reitlinger (physics). He also audits lectures by Robert Zimmerman on aesthetics and Franz Brentano on philosophy. During this year he begins his friendship with Moritz Zitter (1861-1921), who will help support him financially when he is in Berlin.

1880:   Rudolf Steiner attends lectures on Schiller and Goethe by Karl Julius Schröer, who becomes his mentor. Also "through a remarkable combination of circumstances," he meets Felix Koguzki, an "herb gatherer" and healer, who could "see deeply into the secrets of nature." Rudolf Steiner will meet and study with this "emissary of the Master" throughout his time in Vienna.

1881:   January: "... I didn't sleep a wink. I was busy with philosophical problems until about 12:30 a.m. Then, finally, I threw myself down on my couch. All my striving during the previous year had been to research whether the following statement by Schelling was true or not: *Within everyone dwells a secret, marvelous capacity to draw back from the stream of time—out of the self clothed in all that comes to us from outside—into our innermost being and there, in the immutable form of the Eternal, to look into ourselves.* I believe, and I am still quite certain of it, that I discovered this capacity in myself; I had long had an inkling of it. Now the whole of idealist philosophy stood before me in modified form. What's a sleepless night compared to that!"

Rudolf Steiner begins communicating with leading thinkers of the day, who send him books in return, which he reads eagerly.

July: "I am not one of those who dives into the day like an animal in human form. I pursue a quite specific goal, an idealistic aim—knowledge of the truth! This cannot be done offhandedly. It requires the greatest striving in the world, free of all egotism, and equally of all resignation."

August: Steiner puts down on paper for the first time thoughts for a "Philosophy of Freedom." "The striving for the absolute: this human yearning is freedom." He also seeks to outline a "peasant philosophy," describing what the worldview of a "peasant"—one who lives close to the earth and the old ways—really is.

1881-1882: Felix Koguzki, the herb gatherer, reveals himself to be the envoy of another, higher initiatory personality, who instructs Rudolf Steiner to penetrate Fichte's philosophy and to master modern scientific thinking as a preparation for right entry into the spirit. This "Master" also teaches him the double (evolutionary and involutionary) nature of time.

1882: Through the offices of Karl Julius Schröer, Rudolf Steiner is asked by Joseph Kurschner to edit Goethe's scientific works for the *Deutschen National-Literatur* edition. He writes "A Possible Critique of Atomistic Concepts" and sends it to Friedrich Theodore Vischer.

1883: Rudolf Steiner completes his college studies and begins work on the Goethe project.

1884: First volume of Goethe's *Scientific Writings* (CW 1) appears (March). He lectures on Goethe and Lessing, and Goethe's approach to science. In July, he enters the household of Ladislaus and Pauline Specht as tutor to the four Specht boys. He will live there until 1890. At this time, he meets Josef Breuer (1842-1925), the coauthor with Sigmund Freud of *Studies in Hysteria*, who is the Specht family doctor.

1885: While continuing to edit Goethe's writings, Rudolf Steiner reads deeply in contemporary philosophy (Edouard von Hartmann, Johannes Volkelt, and Richard Wahle, among others).

1886: May: Rudolf Steiner sends Kurschner the manuscript of *Outlines of Goethe's Theory of Knowledge* (CW 2), which appears in October, and which he sends out widely. He also meets the poet Marie Eugenie Delle Grazie and writes "Nature and Our Ideals" for her. He attends her salon, where he meets many priests, theologians, and philosophers, who will become his friends. Meanwhile, the director of the Goethe Archive in Weimar requests his collaboration with the *Sophien* edition of Goethe's works, particularly the writings on color.

1887:   At the beginning of the year, Rudolf Steiner is very sick. As the year progresses and his health improves, he becomes increasingly "a man of letters," lecturing, writing essays, and taking part in Austrian cultural life. In August-September, the second volume of Goethe's *Scientific Writings* appears.

1888:   January-July: Rudolf Steiner assumes editorship of the "German Weekly" (*Deutsche Wochenschrift*). He begins lecturing more intensively, giving, for example, a lecture titled "Goethe as Father of a New Aesthetics." He meets and becomes soul friends with Friedrich Eckstein (1861-1939), a vegetarian, philosopher of symbolism, alchemist, and musician, who will introduce him to various spiritual currents (including Theosophy) and with whom he will meditate and interpret esoteric and alchemical texts.

1889:   Rudolf Steiner first reads Nietzsche (*Beyond Good and Evil*). He encounters Theosophy again and learns of Madame Blavatsky in the Theosophical circle around Marie Lang (1858-1934). Here he also meets well-known figures of Austrian life, as well as esoteric figures like the occultist Franz Hartman and Karl Leinigen-Billigen (translator of C.G. Harrison's *The Transcendental Universe*.) During this period, Steiner first reads A.P. Sinnett's *Esoteric Buddhism* and Mabel Collins's *Light on the Path*. He also begins traveling, visiting Budapest, Weimar, and Berlin (where he meets philosopher Edouard von Hartman).

1890:   Rudolf Steiner finishes volume 3 of Goethe's scientific writings. He begins his doctoral dissertation, which will become *Truth and Science* (CW 3). He also meets the poet and feminist Rosa Mayreder (1858-1938), with whom he can exchange his most intimate thoughts. In September, Rudolf Steiner moves to Weimar to work in the Goethe-Schiller Archive.

1891:   Volume 3 of the Kurschner edition of Goethe appears. Meanwhile, Rudolf Steiner edits Goethe's studies in mineralogy and scientific writings for the *Sophien* edition. He meets Ludwig Laistner of the Cotta Publishing Company, who asks for a book on the basic question of metaphysics. From this will result, ultimately, *The Philosophy of Freedom* (CW 4), which will be published not by Cotta but by Emil Felber. In October, Rudolf Steiner takes the oral exam for a doctorate in philosophy, mathematics, and mechanics at Rostock University, receiving his doctorate on the twenty-sixth. In November, he gives his first lecture on Goethe's "Fairy Tale" in Vienna.

1892:   Rudolf Steiner continues work at the Goethe-Schiller Archive and on his *Philosophy of Freedom*. *Truth and Science*, his doctoral dissertation, is published. Steiner undertakes to write introductions to books on Schopenhauer and Jean Paul for Cotta. At year's end, he finds lodging with Anna Eunike, née Schulz (1853-1911), a widow with four daughters and a son. He also develops a friendship with Otto Erich Hartleben (1864-1905) with whom he shares literary interests.

1893: Rudolf Steiner begins his habit of producing many reviews and articles. In March, he gives a lecture titled "Hypnotism, with Reference to Spiritism." In September, volume 4 of the Kurschner edition is completed. In November, *The Philosophy of Freedom* appears. This year, too, he meets John Henry Mackay (1864-1933), the anarchist, and Max Stirner, a scholar and biographer.

1894: Rudolf Steiner meets Elisabeth Förster Nietzsche, the philosopher's sister, and begins to read Nietzsche in earnest, beginning with the as yet unpublished *Antichrist*. He also meets Ernst Haeckel (1834-1919). In the fall, he begins to write *Nietzsche, A Fighter against His Time* (CW 5).

1895: May, *Nietzsche, A Fighter against His Time* appears.

1896: January 22: Rudolf Steiner sees Friedrich Nietzsche for the first and only time. Moves between the Nietzsche and the Goethe-Schiller Archives, where he completes his work before year's end. He falls out with Elisabeth Förster Nietzsche, thus ending his association with the Nietzsche Archive.

1897: Rudolf Steiner finishes the manuscript of *Goethe's Worldview* (CW 6). He moves to Berlin with Anna Eunike and begins editorship of the *Magazin fur Literatur*. From now on, Steiner will write countless reviews, literary and philosophical articles, and so on. He begins lecturing at the "Free Literary Society." In September, he attends the Zionist Congress in Basel. He sides with Dreyfus in the Dreyfus affair.

1898: Rudolf Steiner is very active as an editor in the political, artistic, and theatrical life of Berlin. He becomes friendly with John Henry Mackay and poet Ludwig Jacobowski (1868-1900). He joins Jacobowski's circle of writers, artists, and scientists—"The Coming Ones" (*Die Kommenden*)—and contributes lectures to the group until 1903. He also lectures at the "League for College Pedagogy." He writes an article for Goethe's sesquicentennial, "Goethe's Secret Revelation," on the "Fairy Tale of the Green Snake and the Beautiful Lily."

1888-89: "This was a trying time for my soul as I looked at Christianity. . . . I was able to progress only by contemplating, by means of spiritual perception, the evolution of Christianity . . . . Conscious knowledge of real Christianity began to dawn in me around the turn of the century. This seed continued to develop. My soul trial occurred shortly before the beginning of the twentieth century. It was decisive for my soul's development that I stood spiritually before the Mystery of Golgotha in a deep and solemn celebration of knowledge."

1899: Rudolf Steiner begins teaching and giving lectures and lecture cycles at the Workers' College, founded by Wilhelm Liebknecht (1826-1900). He will continue to do so until 1904. Writes: *Literature and Spiritual Life in the Nineteenth Century; Individualism in Philosophy; Haeckel and His Opponents; Poetry in the Present;* and begins what will become (fifteen years later). *The Riddles of Philosophy* (CW 18). He also meets many artists and writers, including Käthe Kollwitz, Stefan

Zweig, and Rainer Maria Rilke. On October 31, he marries Anna Eunike.

1900: "I thought that the turn of the century must bring humanity a new light. It seemed to me that the separation of human thinking and willing from the spirit had peaked. A turn or reversal of direction in human evolution seemed to me a necessity." Rudolf Steiner finishes *World and Life Views in the Nineteenth Century* (the second part of what will become *The Riddles of Philosophy*) and dedicates it to Ernst Haeckel. It is published in March. He continues lecturing at *Die Kommenden*, whose leadership he assumes after the death of Jacobowski. Also, he gives the Gutenberg Jubilee lecture before 7,000 typesetters and printers. In September, Rudolf Steiner is invited by Count and Countess Brockdorff to lecture in the Theosophical Library. His first lecture is on Nietzsche. His second lecture is titled "Goethe's Secret Revelation." October 6, he begins a lecture cycle on the mystics that will become *Mystics after Modernism* (CW 7). November-December: "Marie von Sivers appears in the audience...." Also in November, Steiner gives his first lecture at the Giordano Bruno Bund (where he will continue to lecture until May, 1905). He speaks on Bruno and modern Rome, focusing on the importance of the philosophy of Thomas Aquinas as monism.

1901: In continual financial straits, Rudolf Steiner's early friends Moritz Zitter and Rosa Mayreder help support him. In October, he begins the lecture cycle *Christianity as Mystical Fact* (CW 8) at the Theosophical Library. In November, he gives his first "Theosophical lecture" on Goethe's "Fairy Tale" in Hamburg at the invitation of Wilhelm Hubbe-Schleiden. He also attends a tea to celebrate the founding of the Theosophical Society at Count and Countess Brockdorff's. He gives a lecture cycle, "From Buddha to Christ," for the circle of the *Kommenden*. November 17, Marie von Sivers asks Rudolf Steiner if Theosophy does not need a Western-Christian spiritual movement (to complement Theosophy's Eastern emphasis). "The question was posed. Now, following spiritual laws, I could begin to give an answer...." In December, Rudolf Steiner writes his first article for a Theosophical publication. At year's end, the Brockdorffs and possibly Wilhelm Hubbe-Schleiden ask Rudolf Steiner to join the Theosophical Society and undertake the leadership of the German section. Rudolf Steiner agrees, on the condition that Marie von Sivers (then in Italy) work with him.

1902: Beginning in January, Rudolf Steiner attends the opening of the Workers' School in Spandau with Rosa Luxemburg (1870-1919). January 17, Rudolf Steiner joins the Theosophical Society. In April, he is asked to become general secretary of the German Section of the Theosophical Society, and works on preparations for its founding. In July, he visits London for a Theosophical congress. He meets Bertram

Keightly, G.R.S. Mead, A.P. Sinnett, and Annie Besant, among others. In September, *Christianity as Mystical Fact* appears. In October, Rudolf Steiner gives his first public lecture on Theosophy ("Monism and Theosophy") to about three hundred people at the Giordano Bruno Bund. On October 19-21, the German Section of the Theosophical Society has its first meeting; Rudolf Steiner is the general secretary, and Annie Besant attends. Steiner lectures on practical karma studies. On October 23, Annie Besant inducts Rudolf Steiner into the Esoteric School of the Theosophical Society. On October 25, Steiner begins a weekly series of lectures: "The Field of Theosophy." During this year, Rudolf Steiner also first meets Ita Wegman (1876-1943), who will become his close collaborator in his final years.

1903: Rudolf Steiner holds about 300 lectures and seminars. In May, the first issue of the periodical *Luzifer* appears. In June, Rudolf Steiner visits London for the first meeting of the Federation of the European Sections of the Theosophical Society, where he meets Colonel Olcott. He begins to write *Theosophy* (CW 9).

1904: Rudolf Steiner continues lecturing at the Workers' College and elsewhere (about 90 lectures), while lecturing intensively all over Germany among Theosophists (about a 140 lectures). In February, he meets Carl Unger (1878-1929), who will become a member of the board of the Anthroposophical Society (1913). In March, he meets Michael Bauer (1871-1929), a Christian mystic, who will also be on the board. In May, *Theosophy* appears, with the dedication: "To the spirit of Giordano Bruno." Rudolf Steiner and Marie von Sivers visit London for meetings with Annie Besant. June: Rudolf Steiner and Marie von Sivers attend the meeting of the Federation of European Sections of the Theosophical Society in Amsterdam. In July, Steiner begins the articles in *Luzifer-Gnosis* that will become *How to Know Higher Worlds* (CW 10) and *Cosmic Memory* (CW 11). In September, Annie Besant visits Germany. In December, Steiner lectures on Freemasonry. He mentions the High Grade Masonry derived from John Yarker and represented by Theodore Reuss and Karl Kellner as a blank slate "into which a good image could be placed."

1905: This year, Steiner ends his non-Theosophical lecturing activity. Supported by Marie von Sivers, his Theosophical lecturing—both in public and in the Theosophical Society—increases significantly: "The German Theosophical Movement is of exceptional importance." Steiner recommends reading, among others, Fichte, Jacob Boehme, and Angelus Silesius. He begins to introduce Christian themes into Theosophy. He also begins to work with doctors (Felix Peipers and Ludwig Noll). In July, he is in London for the Federation of European Sections, where he attends a lecture by Annie Besant: "I have seldom seen Mrs. Besant speak in so inward and heartfelt a manner...." "Through Mrs. Besant I have found the way to H.P. Blavatsky."

September to October, he gives a course of thirty-one lectures for a small group of esoteric students. In October, the annual meeting of the German Section of the Theosophical Society, which still remains very small, takes place. Rudolf Steiner reports membership has risen from 121 to 377 members. In November, seeking to establish esoteric "continuity," Rudolf Steiner and Marie von Sivers participate in a "Memphis-Misraim" Masonic ceremony. They pay forty-five marks for membership. "Yesterday, you saw how little remains of former esoteric institutions." "We are dealing only with a 'framework'… for the present, nothing lies behind it. The occult powers have completely withdrawn."

1906: Expansion of Theosophical work. Rudolf Steiner gives about 245 lectures, only 44 of which take place in Berlin. Cycles are given in Paris, Leipzig, Stuttgart, and Munich. Esoteric work also intensifies. Rudolf Steiner begins writing *An Outline of Esoteric Science* (CW 13). In January, Rudolf Steiner receives permission (a patent) from the Great Orient of the Scottish A & A Thirty-Three Degree Rite of the Order of the Ancient Freemasons of the Memphis-Misraim Rite to direct a chapter under the name "Mystica Aeterna." This will become the "Cognitive Cultic Section" (also called "Misraim Service") of the Esoteric School. (See: *From the History and Contents of the Cognitive Cultic Section* (CW 264). During this time, Steiner also meets Albert Schweitzer. In May, he is in Paris, where he visits Edouard Schuré. Many Russians attend his lectures (including Konstantin Balmont, Dimitri Mereszkovski, Zinaida Hippius, and Maximilian Woloshin). He attends the General Meeting of the European Federation of the Theosophical Society, at which Col. Olcott is present for the last time. He spends the year's end in Venice and Rome, where he writes and works on his translation of H.P. Blavatsky's *Key to Theosophy*.

1907: Further expansion of the German Theosophical Movement according to the Rosicrucian directive to "introduce spirit into the world"—in education, in social questions, in art, and in science. In February, Col. Olcott dies in Adyar. Before he dies, Olcott indicates that "the Masters" wish Annie Besant to succeed him: much politicking ensues. Rudolf Steiner supports Besant's candidacy. April-May: preparations for the Congress of the Federation of European Sections of the Theosophical Society—the great, watershed Whitsun "Munich Congress," attended by Annie Besant and others. Steiner decides to separate Eastern and Western (Christian-Rosicrucian) esoteric schools. He takes his esoteric school out of the Theosophical Society (Besant and Rudolf Steiner are "in harmony" on this). Steiner makes his first lecture tours to Austria and Hungary. That summer, he is in Italy. In September, he visits Edouard Schuré, who will write the introduction to the French edition of *Christianity as Mystical Fact* in Barr, Alsace. Rudolf Steiner writes the autobiographical statement known as the "Barr Document." In *Luzifer–Gnosis*, "The Education of the Child" appears.

1908: The movement grows (membership: 1150). Lecturing expands. Steiner makes his first extended lecture tour to Holland and Scandinavia, as well as visits to Naples and Sicily. Themes: St. John's Gospel, the Apocalypse, Egypt, science, philosophy, and logic. *Luzifer-Gnosis* ceases publication. In Berlin, Marie von Sivers (with Johanna Mücke (1864-1949) forms the *Philosophisch-Theosophisch* (after 1915 *Philosophisch-Anthroposophisch*) *Verlag* to publish Steiner's work. Steiner gives lecture cycles titled *The Gospel of St. John* (CW 103) and *The Apocalypse* (104).

1909: *An Outline of Esoteric Science* appears. Lecturing and travel continues. Rudolf Steiner's spiritual research expands to include the polarity of Lucifer and Ahriman; the work of great individualities in history; the Maitreya Buddha and the Bodhisattvas; spiritual economy (CW 109); the work of the spiritual hierarchies in heaven and on Earth (CW 110). He also deepens and intensifies his research into the Gospels, giving lectures on the Gospel of St. Luke (CW 114) with the first mention of two Jesus children. Meets and becomes friends with Christian Morgenstern (1871-1914). In April, he lays the foundation stone for the Malsch model—the building that will lead to the first Goetheanum. In May, the International Congress of the Federation of European Sections of the Theosophical Society takes place in Budapest. Rudolf Steiner receives the Subba Row medal for *How to Know Higher Worlds*. During this time, Charles W. Leadbeater discovers Jiddu Krishnamurti (1895-1986) and proclaims him the future "world teacher," the bearer of the Maitreya Buddha and the "reappearing Christ." In October, Steiner delivers seminal lectures on "anthroposophy," which he will try, unsuccessfully, to rework over the next years into the unfinished work, *Anthroposophy (A Fragment)* (CW 45).

1910: New themes: *The Reappearance of Christ in the Etheric* (CW 118); *The Fifth Gospel; The Mission of Folk Souls* (CW 121); *Occult History* (CW 126); the evolving development of etheric cognitive capacities. Rudolf Steiner continues his Gospel research with *The Gospel of St. Matthew* (CW 123). In January, his father dies. In April, he takes a month-long trip to Italy, including Rome, Monte Cassino, and Sicily. He also visits Scandinavia again. July-August, he writes the first mystery drama, *The Portal of Initiation* (CW 14). In November, he gives "psychosophy" lectures. In December, he submits "On the Psychological Foundations and Epistemological Framework of Theosophy" to the International Philosophical Congress in Bologna.

1911: The crisis in the Theosophical Society deepens. In January, "The Order of the Rising Sun," which will soon become "The Order of the Star in the East," is founded for the coming world teacher, Krishnamurti. At the same time, Marie von Sivers, Rudolf Steiner's coworker, falls ill. Fewer lectures are given, but important new ground is broken. In Prague, in March, Steiner meets Franz Kafka (1883-1924) and Hugo Bergmann (1883-1975). In April, he delivers his paper to the

Philosophical Congress. He writes the second mystery drama, *The Soul's Probation* (CW 14). Also, while Marie von Sivers is convalescing, Rudolf Steiner begins work on *Calendar 1912/1913*, which will contain the "Calendar of the Soul" meditations. On March 19, Anna (Eunike) Steiner dies. In September, Rudolf Steiner visits Einsiedeln, birthplace of Paracelsus. In December, Friedrich Rittelmeyer, future founder of the Christian Community, meets Rudolf Steiner. The *Johannes-Bauverein*, the "building committee," which would lead to the first Goetheanum (first planned for Munich), is also founded, and a preliminary committee for the founding of an independent association is created that, in the following year, will become the Anthroposophical Society. Important lecture cycles include *Occult Physiology* (CW 128); *Wonders of the World* (CW 129); *From Jesus to Christ* (CW 131). Other themes: esoteric Christianity; Christian Rosenkreutz; the spiritual guidance of humanity; the sense world and the world of the spirit.

1912:   Despite the ongoing, now increasing crisis in the Theosophical Society, much is accomplished: *Calendar 1912/1913* is published; eurythmy is created; both the third mystery drama, *The Guardian of the Threshold* (CW 14) and *A Way of Self-Knowledge* (CW 16) are written. New (or renewed) themes included life between death and rebirth and karma and reincarnation. Other lecture cycles: *Spiritual Beings in the Heavenly Bodies and the Kingdoms of Nature* (CW 136); *The Human Being in the Light of Occultism, Theosophy, and Philosophy* (CW 137); *The Gospel of St. Mark* (CW 139); and *The Bhagavad Gita and the Epistles of Paul* (CW 142). On May 8, Rudolf Steiner celebrates White Lotus Day, H.P. Blavatsky's death day, which he had faithfully observed for the past decade, for the last time. In August, Rudolf Steiner suggests the "independent association" be called the "Anthroposophical Society." In September, the first eurythmy course takes place. In October, Rudolf Steiner declines recognition of a Theosophical Society lodge dedicated to the Star of the East and decides to expel all Theosophical Society members belonging to the order. Also, with Marie von Sivers, he first visits Dornach, near Basel, Switzerland, and they stand on the hill where the Goetheanum will be. In November, a Theosophical Society lodge is opened by direct mandate from Adyar (Annie Besant). In December, a meeting of the German section occurs at which it is decided that belonging to the Order of the Star of the East is incompatible with membership in the Theosophical Society. December 28: informal founding of the Anthroposophical Society in Berlin.

1913:   Expulsion of the German section from the Theosophical Society. February 2-3: Foundation meeting of the Anthroposophical Society. Board members include: Marie von Sivers, Michael Bauer, and Carl Unger. September 20: Laying of the foundation stone for the *Johannes Bau* (Goetheanum) in Dornach. Building begins immediately. The third mystery drama, *The Soul's Awakening* (CW 14), is completed.

Also: *The Threshold of the Spiritual World* (CW 147). Lecture cycles include: *The Bhagavad Gita and the Epistles of Paul* and *The Esoteric Meaning of the Bhagavad Gita* (CW 146), which the Russian philosopher Nikolai Berdyaev attends; *The Mysteries of the East and of Christianity* (CW 144); *The Effects of Esoteric Development* (CW 145); and *The Fifth Gospel* (CW 148). In May, Rudolf Steiner is in London and Paris, where anthroposophical work continues.

1914: Building continues on the *Johannes Bau* (Goetheanum) in Dornach, with artists and coworkers from seventeen nations. The general assembly of the Anthroposophical Society takes place. In May, Rudolf Steiner visits Paris, as well as Chartres Cathedral. June 28: assassination in Sarajevo ("Now the catastrophe has happened!"). August 1: War is declared. Rudolf Steiner returns to Germany from Dornach—he will travel back and forth. He writes the last chapter of *The Riddles of Philosophy*. Lecture cycles include: *Human and Cosmic Thought* (CW 151); *Inner Being of Humanity between Death and a New Birth* (CW 153); *Occult Reading and Occult Hearing* (CW 156). December 24: marriage of Rudolf Steiner and Marie von Sivers.

1915: Building continues. Life after death becomes a major theme, also art. Writes: *Thoughts during a Time of War* (CW 24). Lectures include: *The Secret of Death* (CW 159); *The Uniting of Humanity through the Christ Impulse* (CW 165).

1916: Rudolf Steiner begins work with Edith Maryon (1872-1924) on the sculpture "The Representative of Humanity" ("The Group"—Christ, Lucifer, and Ahriman). He also works with the alchemist Alexander von Bernus on the quarterly *Das Reich*. He writes *The Riddle of Humanity* (CW 20). Lectures include: *Necessity and Freedom in World History and Human Action* (CW 166); *Past and Present in the Human Spirit* (CW 167); *The Karma of Vocation* (CW 172); *The Karma of Untruthfulness* (CW 173).

1917: Russian Revolution. The U.S. enters the war. Building continues. Rudolf Steiner delineates the idea of the "threefold nature of the human being" (in a public lecture March 15) and the "threefold nature of the social organism" (hammered out in May-June with the help of Otto von Lerchenfeld and Ludwig Polzer-Hoditz in the form of two documents titled *Memoranda*, which were distributed in high places). August-September: Rudolf Steiner writes *The Riddles of the Soul* (CW 20). Also: commentary on "The Chemical Wedding of Christian Rosenkreutz" for Alexander Bernus (*Das Reich*). Lectures include: *The Karma of Materialism* (CW 176); *The Spiritual Background of the Outer World: The Fall of the Spirits of Darkness* (CW 177).

1918: March 18: peace treaty of Brest-Litovsk—"Now everything will truly enter chaos! What is needed is cultural renewal." June: Rudolf Steiner visits Karlstein (Grail) Castle outside Prague. Lecture cycle: *From Symptom to Reality in Modern History* (CW 185). In mid-November,

Emil Molt, of the Waldorf-Astoria Cigarette Company, has the idea of founding a school for his workers' children.

1919:   Focus on the threefold social organism: tireless travel, countless lectures, meetings, and publications. At the same time, a new public stage of Anthroposophy emerges as cultural renewal begins. The coming years will see initiatives in pedagogy, medicine, pharmacology, and agriculture. January 27: threefold meeting: " We must first of all, with the money we have, found free schools that can bring people what they need." February: first public eurythmy performance in Zurich. Also: "Appeal to the German People" (CW 24), circulated March 6 as a newspaper insert. In April, *Toward Social Renewal* (CW 23)—"perhaps the most widely read of all books on politics appearing since the war"—appears. Rudolf Steiner is asked to undertake the "direction and leadership" of the school founded by the Waldorf-Astoria Company. Rudolf Steiner begins to talk about the "renewal" of education. May 30: a building is selected and purchased for the future Waldorf School. August-September, Rudolf Steiner gives a lecture course for Waldorf teachers, *The Foundations of Human Experience (Study of Man)* (CW 293). September 7: Opening of the first Waldorf School. December (into January): first science course, the *Light Course* (CW 320).

1920:   The Waldorf School flourishes. New threefold initiatives. Founding of limited companies *Der Kommenden Tag* and *Futurum A.G.* to infuse spiritual values into the economic realm. Rudolf Steiner also focuses on the sciences. Lectures: *Introducing Anthroposophical Medicine* (CW 312); *The Warmth Course* (CW 321); *The Boundaries of Natural Science* (CW 322); *The Redemption of Thinking* (CW 74). February: Johannes Werner Klein—later a cofounder of the Christian Community—asks Rudolf Steiner about the possibility of a "religious renewal," a "Johannine church." In March, Rudolf Steiner gives the first course for doctors and medical students. In April, a divinity student asks Rudolf Steiner a second time about the possibility of religious renewal. September 27-October 16: anthroposophical "university course." December: lectures titled *The Search for the New Isis* (CW 202).

1921:   Rudolf Steiner continues his intensive work on cultural renewal, including the uphill battle for the threefold social order. "University" arts, scientific, theological, and medical courses include: *The Astronomy Course* (CW 323); *Observation, Mathematics, and Scientific Experiment* (CW 324); the *Second Medical Course* (CW 313); *Color.* In June and September-October, Rudolf Steiner also gives the first two "priests' courses" (CW 342 and 343). The "youth movement" gains momentum. Magazines are founded: *Die Drei* (January), and—under the editorship of Albert Steffen (1884-1963)—the weekly, *Das Goetheanum* (August). In February-March, Rudolf Steiner takes his first trip outside Germany since the war (Holland). On April 7, Steiner receives a letter regarding "religious renewal," and May 22-23, he agrees to address the question in a practical way. In June, the Klinical-Therapeutic Institute opens in Arlesheim under the direction of Dr. Ita Wegman. In August, the Chemical-Pharmaceutical Laboratory opens in Arlesheim (Oskar Schmiedel and Ita Wegman, directors). The Clinical Therapeutic Institute is inaugurated in Stuttgart (Dr. Ludwig Noll, director); also the Research Laboratory in Dornach (Ehrenfried Pfeiffer and Gunther Wachsmuth, directors). In November-December, Rudolf Steiner visits Norway.

1922:   The first half of the year involves very active public lecturing (thousands attend); in the second half, Rudolf Steiner begins to withdraw and turn toward the Society—"The Society is asleep." It is "too weak" to do what is asked of it. The businesses—*Die Kommenden Tag* and *Futura A.G.*—fail. In January, with the help of an agent, Steiner undertakes a twelve-city German tour, accompanied by eurythmy performances. In two weeks he speaks to more than 2,000 people. In April, he gives a "university course" in The Hague. He also visits England. In June, he is in Vienna for the East-West Congress. In August-September, he is back in England for the Oxford Conference on Education. Returning to Dornach, he gives the lectures *Philosophy, Cosmology, and Religion* (CW 215), and gives the third priest's course (CW 344). On September 16, The Christian Community is founded. In October-November, Steiner is in Holland and England. He also speaks to the youth: *The Youth Course* (CW 217). In December, Steiner gives lectures titled *The Origins of Natural Science* (CW 326), and *Humanity and the World of Stars: The Spiritual Communion of Humanity* (CW 219). December 31: Fire at the Goetheanum, which is destroyed.

1923:   Despite the fire, Rudolf Steiner continues his work unabated. A very hard year. Internal dispersion, dissension, and apathy abound. There is conflict—between old and new visions—within the society. A wake-up call is needed, and Rudolf Steiner responds with renewed lecturing vitality. His focus: the spiritual context of human life; initiation science; the course of the year; and community building. As a foundation for an artistic school, he creates a series of pastel sketches. Lecture cycles: *The Anthroposophical Movement; Initiation Science* (CW 227) (in England at the Penmaenmawr Summer School); *The Four Seasons and the Archangels* (CW 229); *Harmony of the Creative Word* (CW 230); *The Supersensible Human* (CW 231), given in Holland for the founding of the Dutch society. On November 10, in response to the failed Hitler-Ludendorf putsch in Munich, Steiner closes his Berlin residence and moves the *Philosophisch-Anthroposophisch Verlag* (Press) to Dornach. On December 9, Steiner begins the serialization of his *Autobiography: The Course of My Life* (CW 28) in *Das Goetheanum*. It will continue to appear weekly, without a break, until his death. Late December-early January: Rudolf Steiner refounds the Anthroposophical Society (about 12,000 members internationally) and takes over its leadership. The new board members are: Marie Steiner, Ita Wegman, Albert Steffen, Elizabeth Vreede, and Guenther Wachsmuth. (See *The Christmas Meeting for the Founding of the General Anthroposophical Society* (CW 260). Accompanying lectures: *Mystery Knowledge and Mystery Centers* (CW 232); *World History in the Light of Anthroposophy* (CW 233). December 25: the Foundation Stone is laid (in the hearts of members) in the form of the "Foundation Stone Meditation."

1924:   January 1: having founded the Anthroposophical Society and taken over its leadership, Rudolf Steiner has the task of "reforming" it. The process begins with a weekly newssheet ("What's Happening in the Anthroposophical Society") in which Rudolf Steiner's "Letters to Members" and "Anthroposophical Leading Thoughts" appear (CW 26). The next step is the creation of a new esoteric class, the "first class" of the "University of Spiritual Science" (which was to have been followed, had Rudolf Steiner lived longer, by two more advanced classes). Then comes a new language for Anthroposophy—practical, phenomenological, and direct; and Rudolf Steiner creates the model for the second Goetheanum. He begins the series of extensive "karma" lectures (CW 235-40); and finally, responding to needs, he creates two new initiatives: biodynamic agriculture and curative education. After the middle of the year, rumors begin to circulate regarding Steiner's health. Lectures: January-February, *Anthroposophy* (CW 234); February: *Tone Eurythmy* (CW 278); June: *The Agriculture Course* (CW 327); June-July: Speech [?] Eurythmy (CW 279); *Curative Education* (CW 317); August: (England, "Second International Summer School"), *Initiation Consciousness: True and False Paths in Spiritual Investigation* (CW 243); September: *Pastoral Medicine* (CW 318). On September 26, for the first time, Rudolf Steiner cancels a lecture. On September 28, he gives his last lecture. On September 29, he withdraws to his studio in the carpenter's shop; now he is definitively ill. Cared for by Ita Wegman, he continues working, however, and writing the weekly installments of his *Autobiography* and *Letters to the Members/Leading Thoughts* (CW 26).

1925:   Rudolf Steiner, while continuing to work, continues to weaken. He finishes *Extending Practical Medicine* (CW 27) with Ita Wegman. On March 30, around ten in the morning, Rudolf Steiner dies.

INDEX